Leadership in the Era of AI

What will be the right place for humans in the new economy of AI, avatars, automation, and 3D virtual worlds? Our job will be to bring wisdom to our workplace and the marketplace, working with intelligent machines, and this book is the roadmap.

Though it addresses growing fears about the future of work, The Future of Leadership is about more than specific technologies. It's about building organizational intelligence (OI): the capability of an organization to comprehend and create knowledge relevant to its purpose. To increase organizational intelligence requires a new kind of knowledge worker – a wisdom worker – who requires a new kind of leadership. Written in an engaging business novel format, this book is the story of how to become a leader of wisdom workers and be successful in the emerging wisdom economy.

Seasoned and emerging leaders in all industries, as well as talent development professionals, will value this book's insights into how to step confidently into the developing work paradigm, bringing human values and wisdom together with the latest AI in the real and virtual worlds.

Mark Salisbury is a computer scientist, professor, leader, speaker, author, consultant, and expert on the future. He is a professor of Computer Science and Organizational Development and Change at the University of St. Thomas. Mark's previous books are *iLearning: How to Create an Innovative Learning Organization* and *Socrates Digital™ for Learning and Problem Solving*.

Leadership in the Era of AI

How to Grow Organizational Intelligence

Mark Salisbury

NEW YORK AND LONDON

Designed cover image: iStock

First published 2025
by Routledge
605 Third Avenue, New York, NY 10158

and by Routledge
4 Park Square, Milton Park, Abingdon, Oxon, OX14 4RN

Routledge is an imprint of the Taylor & Francis Group, an informa business

ISBN: 9781032828374 (hbk)
ISBN: 9781032820712 (pbk)
ISBN: 9781003506591 (ebk)

DOI: 10.4324/9781003506591

Typeset in Times New Roman
by codeMantra

For my parents, Woodford & Leola, who taught me the most important things in life

Contents

Figures

Acknowledgments

I have many people to thank for their help with this book. First, I want to thank David Olson for introducing me to the world of computing so long ago. My life was forever changed.

I thank Ann List, who took on the job of editing an early manuscript for this work. Ann not only fixed typos, filled in omissions, and corrected grammatical mistakes, but also helped me clarify the wording and the underlying message of the book.

I also thank Kevin Brady, Bob Grassberger, and Bill Meador from the University of New Mexico for sharing their ideas, resources, and interest in the *wisdom economy* with me. They have been my "community of practice" for this work.

Thanks to Meredith Norwich, my acquisitions editor, for her willingness to take a chance on an "unconventional book."

I wish to thank my literary agent, Jeff Herman, for his help in bringing this book into the light of day.

Finally, thanks to my wife, Joan, for all her input, love, and support.

About the Author

Mark Salisbury is a computer scientist, professor, leader, speaker, author, consultant, and expert on the future. After completing his PhD at the University of Oregon, Mark worked for 11 years at The Boeing Company where he worked in research and development in the field of artificial intelligence. After leaving Boeing, Mark founded Vitel, Inc., a knowledge management solution provider for the U.S. Department of Energy and the National Laboratories. Mark was also a professor and program director at the University of New Mexico for 17 years where he published extensively in artificial intelligence and knowledge management. Finally, Mark has been the dean of the College of Education, Leadership, and Counseling at the University of St. Thomas. Currently, he is a professor of Computer Science and Organizational Development and Change at the University of St. Thomas. Mark's previous books are *iLearning: How to Create an Innovative Learning Organization*, published by Wiley in 2009, and *Socrates Digital™ for Learning and Problem Solving*, published by IGI-Global in 2022.

Preface

Why Is This Book Important?

The arrival of artificially intelligent avatars and the automation they bring are worrying many of us, not only for our livelihood but also for the jobs that may be lost to our kids. We worry about what our place will be as human beings in this new economy where much of it will be conducted online in the metaverse – in a network of 3D virtual worlds – working with intelligent machines. *Leadership in the Era of AI* was written to address these fears and show what our place will be – the right place – in this new economy of AI avatars, automation, and 3D virtual worlds. But to be successful in this new economy, our job will be to bring wisdom to our workplace and the marketplace. And we will use AI avatars and 3D virtual worlds to do it. However, this book is about more than the AI avatars that we will work within the metaverse. It's about how to lead the effort for growing Organizational intelligence (OI) – the capability of an organization to comprehend and create knowledge relevant to its purpose; in other words, it is the intellectual capacity of the entire organization. To increase organizational intelligence requires a new kind of leadership for a new kind of knowledge worker, a *wisdom worker*. This book begins your story for how to become a wisdom worker, lead other wisdom workers, and be successful in the emerging *wisdom economy*.

What Can You Achieve with This Book?

After completing this book, you will be able to do the following:

1 Recognize the characteristics of the new generation of *wisdom workers* and how they differ from their predecessors.
2 Recognize that new leadership methods and techniques are needed to lead this new generation of *wisdom workers.*
3 Apply personal and professional values – personal integrity, belief in something larger than yourself, and keeping the best interest of others in mind – to improve your work performance and lead others.

4 Exhibit an attitude of confidence, courage, and reciprocity of sharing knowledge to increase your productivity and influence others.
5 Leverage artificial intelligence to accelerate your ability to learn, augment your decision-making, and lead others.
6 Utilize new technologies to communicate with human colleagues and intelligent machines to develop better solutions more quickly.

How Is This Book Organized?

Leadership in the Era of AI has five main parts. Part 1 explains why high organizational intelligence requires brains. Part 2 tells why high organizational intelligence requires courage. Part 3 shows why high organizational intelligence requires heart. Part 4 shows how to grow organizational intelligence. And, finally, Part 5 describes how to lead for growing organizational intelligence.

The first part of each chapter reads like a "business novel." It follows two work teams in a company that specializes in providing research and development (R&D) services to other companies. One team has an "old school" boss who controls every aspect of the team. The other team has high organizational intelligence and has become a team of *wisdom workers*. The continuing story about these two teams reveals the profound productivity that teams with high organizational intelligence bring to the workplace and what is required to lead them effectively.

The second half of each chapter is a discussion about the differences between the two teams. It details the underlying reasons for the differences and how those differences play out regarding productivity for the teams. At the end of each chapter, the differences between the teams and the key actions for increasing organizational intelligence are highlighted.

As with the characters in this book, the author acknowledges that AI-based technologies were used to edit some content and takes responsibility that the validity, originality, and integrity of the book are in accordance with the publisher's editorial polices on authorship and principles of publishing ethics.

Introduction

The modern workplace is undergoing a rapid technological evolution during a time of profound human expectations for the future. At the confluence of this transformation is the capacity of people and intelligent machines to create knowledge: Organizational Intelligence. This book delves deep into this idea, weaving together the intricate threads of individual values, collective wisdom, and the symbiotic relationship with intelligent machines.

For many, the traditional work paradigms have revolved around individual competencies and isolated team efforts. However, the emphasis has shifted as our professional environments become more interconnected and complex. No longer is it sufficient to operate in silos; our age demands an understanding and harnessing of the collective intelligence that lies within the heart of an organization. At its core, this collective capacity to create knowledge is the definition of organizational intelligence.

Yet, this concept is more than just reliant on the collective wisdom of human teams. As we progress into the twenty-first century, artificial intelligence and machine learning become intrinsic parts of our professional lives. With their vast data processing capabilities and predictive analytics, intelligent machines are not just tools but partners, amplifying our inherent human potential. This book underscores the importance of forging a harmonious relationship with these machines to elevate our organizational intelligence.

But beyond machines and collective human wisdom, this book also reiterates the timeless importance of personal and professional values. In the interconnected maze of modern workspaces, authenticity and integrity stand out as beacons. Personal integrity, a belief in a purpose greater than oneself, and prioritizing the collective good are not just values but necessities. These pillars ensure the core of organizational intelligence is robust and resilient.

As you journey through these pages, you will encounter characters and narratives that illustrate these ideas, from the pitfalls of leadership like Neil Anderthal's, who operates with a blinkered vision, to the enlightened leadership of Josie Wang, who embodies the ideals of a wisdom worker in the truest sense.

DOI: 10.4324/9781003506591-1

Through their stories, you'll witness the tangible impact of organizational intelligence (or the lack thereof) on work cultures, team dynamics, and overall organizational success.

Furthermore, this book will equip you with actionable insights and promises to yourself, guiding you toward leadership success in this new age of work. These promises are more than just professional commitments; they are a roadmap to personal evolution in sync with the demands of contemporary workplaces.

Part 1

Organizational Intelligence Requires Brains

Chapter 1

Avoid Single Intelligence Leadership

Five Years into the Future...

Wham! The noise startled Anya, and she turned her head.

"I don't care about the binder, but you scared three years of life out of me!" Anya shouted under her breath.

"Sorry, I didn't mean to throw it down that hard," Jake said as he sat down and let out a deep sigh. Anya reached out and put her hand on Jake's shoulder. "It's just that I hate these meetings," he said.

"Maybe, he won't be here today," Anya said cheerfully.

"No, he's here. I saw him posing in the men's bathroom."

Anya leaned into him, "Posing? What do you mean?"

"He looks at himself in the mirror and watches himself while he says something silly like, 'I'm here to help you make your deadlines and be successful,'" Jake said.

They heard the door open and saw the other half dozen members of their team trudge in. "Hi" was said a couple of times in a whisper. The sound of work binders flopping on the table drowned out heavy sighs.

Then the door quickly swung open, and he walked in. He was their boss – Dr. Neil Anderthal. And they were at their weekly team meeting as workers in research and development at Big Time R&D. Their R&D Division had been spun off from the Big Time Company ten years ago. They now performed R&D for many large companies, conglomerates, and the government.

Dr. Anderthal had several handouts under his arm and immediately passed them out.

He paused for the team to look at him. In a booming voice, he said, "The first handout has the yearly goals for Big Time R&D."

Again, Dr. Anderthal paused for a couple of seconds and held up another handout. "This handout has the goals for our team this year," he said.

"And this handout outlines the goals and objectives for a new project we will be taking on," he said as he held up a third document. "It's on developing a new personal transportation device for a large automaker."

DOI: 10.4324/9781003506591-3

The other people in the room, the team members, looked at the handouts and nodded their heads.

Dr. Anderthal continued, "I've created a project schedule with milestones for deliverables. You'll see it at the end of the last handout."

"Note that it has the due dates with the names of the people who have been assigned the deliverables," he added.

"Now, if you cannot make a date for one of your deliverables for any reason – and it had better be a good one – let me know as soon as possible," he said in a loud voice.

Dr. Anderthal straightened up and put his hands on his waist. "You know, I'm here to help you make your deadlines and be successful, so come to me with any problems you may have."

Jake made a smirk that turned into a cough. Dr. Anderthal looked at Jake and raised an eyebrow. Jake raised his arms with his palms up as if to say, "I couldn't help it – a cough snuck up on me."

Dr. Anderthal continued, "If you have proposed adjustments to your deliverables or for the schedule, send it to me and I'll make a ruling on it. That's it."

He concluded with, "We'll meet back here at our usual time next week for your progress reports – and don't forget to send me your PowerPoint slides ahead of time." Then he paused and added, "Oh, and make sure that your work in our project world of the metaverse is up to date."

***

Single Intelligence Leadership

Although they don't know it yet, Anya and Jake are on their way to becoming workers in the wisdom economy. In this new economy (and you heard it here, first), people collaborate to create wisdom with intelligent machines – and other machines act on that wisdom. This dramatic change in work requires a new "brainy" kind of worker – ones who leverage artificial intelligence and use the metaverse to accelerate their ability to learn and solve problems – and share that problem-solving.

As shown in Figure 1.1, first-generation manufacturing workers and managers only needed to think a little to complete their work. Hence, the capability of the organization to comprehend and create knowledge relevant to its purpose was relatively low – which corresponded to low organizational intelligence. Second-generation workers and supervisors require considerable thought to process information and solve problems, resulting in a higher level of organizational intelligence. Peter Drucker coined the term "knowledge worker" to describe these second-generation workers and supervisors.

| Manufacturing Worker | Knowledge Worker | Wisdom Worker |

Figure 1.1 The Evolution of the Wisdom Worker.

However, the new generation of wisdom workers differs entirely from those preceding them. These wisdom workers use technology to accelerate their ability to learn and solve problems, thereby enabling them to create new knowledge at an accelerating rate – the very definition of very high organizational intelligence. Moreover, as we will discuss shortly, it's not only that wisdom workers are different from their predecessors at the individual level, but they are also remarkably different and more productive in the networks they form. Facilitating these powerful and effective networks requires a new kind of leadership.

Figure 1.2 shows the inner workings of a team led by a manufacturing boss. The first thing to note is the hierarchical relationship between the boss and the workers. The next thing to notice is the thick, squiggly lines between the boss and the workers. They are the line of control that the boss uses to assert authority over the workers. The wider the line, the more interactions there are where the boss comes off as giving orders to subordinates. Note that the bosses have the same interactions with their subordinates at the level below the manufacturing boss.

A critical line is the one going from each worker to the boss. Notice how skinny it is in a network of manufacturing workers. These thin lines indicate little flow of information back to the boss. People tell their bosses little of what they have learned – or anyone else. From the perspective of the manufacturing boss, this is not as important as the line of control that the boss uses to ensure things get done. The problem with this perspective is that machines are becoming more

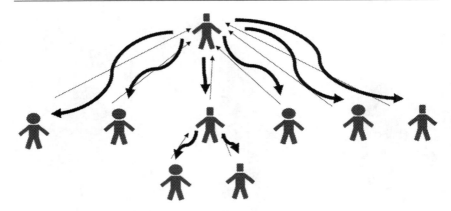

Figure 1.2 Manufacturing Worker Network.

and more capable of getting things done. At the same time, it's becoming more apparent that the actual value of people for organizations is their learning of new knowledge that machines can apply. In a manufacturing worker network, people learn very little new knowledge that is shared and later applied in solving new problems, meaning that manufacturing bosses gain little new knowledge from the people who report to them. All these observations are tell-tale signs of an organization with low organizational intelligence.

Of course, in our story, Neil Anderthal is a manufacturing boss trying to supervise workers in a wisdom economy. As a result, his network looks like a manufacturing worker network. Jake and Anya are two knowledge workers in Anderthal's network of manufacturing workers. They are collaborative by nature and like to learn new things. However, when embedded in a network of manufacturing workers, they act as manufacturing workers who apply little of their thinking to their work. This "command and control" method almost disappeared by the end of the twentieth century. Anderthal and a few others had managed to continue its use, covering up their outdated management style with "politically correct" memos and presentations that made it sound like they were doing collaborative work in their teams.

Figure 1.3 shows the team network created by a manager of knowledge workers. Most organizations in the early part of the twenty-first century still work directly with a similar way of control. Unlike a network of manufacturing workers, the first thing to notice in a knowledge worker network is that everyone reports directly to the manager. No "little managers" form a chain of command as there is for the manager in the manufacturing network. In the knowledge worker network, the manager makes the decisions (or the final decisions based on input or recommendations) for the whole team while promoting a collaborative work environment.

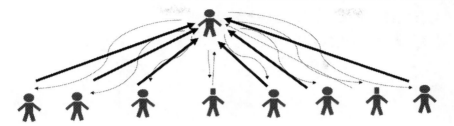

Figure 1.3 Knowledge Worker Network.

The second thing to notice is that the control lines are thinner than those of the previous manufacturer's worker network. The knowledge worker managers behave more like they direct or guide projects while incorporating team members' input. The manager and team understand that the responsibility for the success of a project ultimately rests with the manager, which means that the manager makes the final calls. However, note that there is more flow of information back to the manager than in the previous manufacturer worker network. The increased flow is because the manager is aware of the value of what team members have learned while solving problems in completing a project. Therefore, the manager seeks "best practices" from their team members and "screens" the best ones for storage in the manager's library of best practices.

Overall, the knowledge worker network improves productivity over the manufacturer worker network in the information-based economy. However, it still carries over the significant limitations of the manufacturing worker network. The information that flows back to the manager requires much thought before its use in another project. (Think about using the design documentation from one project for another one. It would take the judgment and knowledge of an expert to "convert" or "reuse" the design documentation for another project.) Also, note that some of the members of the knowledge worker network may behave and produce like they are in a manufacturer worker network – providing little information back to the manager. While the knowledge worker network is more collaborative than the manufacturer worker network, the knowledge worker network is only slightly more productive than the manufacturer worker network.

Chapter 2

Employ Collaborative Leadership

Meanwhile, in a new world in the metaverse, another team is beginning a meeting.

"Looks like I won't be late, after all," said an avatar that was just coming online. It was Josie Wang, the leader of the team – with a box of virtual donuts and coffee. Team members can use the gift certificates to have their own favorite snacks and beverages during team meetings in the metaverse.

"Last time, you were telling us about a moose in your pajamas, Jared," Josie said with a laugh. "We heard the first part of that story last week, but I'm not sure I buy the whole thing!"

After people had a chance to get their coffee and something to eat, they shared news unrelated to work. Of concern to everyone was John's wife. She had been taking chemo treatments, and they hadn't been going well. John reported that she was doing better and told a funny story about mistakenly locking their dog outside.

"Well, thanks for the update, John. We'd better get down to business," Josie said with a smile.

"Last meeting, we discussed and decided to support Luke and Yolanda's idea for a new project in response to a request by the CIA. They gave the new project the codename "Emotional Intelligence Glasses," Josie said. "Since then, I've run the idea past Ajay Gupta, our new Division VP. He talked to the CIA and had their support for it. I also created a metaverse world for this project and developed a budget with Socrates Digital® 1 for it. I hope you have had a chance to ask Socrates Digital® any questions that you may have had about the budget."

"At this meeting, we will work with Socrates Digital® to determine the feasibility of developing Emotional Intelligence Glasses. If turns out that it's feasible, we will put together a strategy for accomplishing the project," Josie continued.

***

DOI: 10.4324/9781003506591-4

Collaborative Leadership

On the surface, it appears the difference between the two teams is that one manager is nicer to work for than the other. Josie Wang is simply a nicer person than Neil Anderthal. But there's much more of a difference than that. Josie's team does the work of three similar teams. That's right. Her team does three times the amount of research and development for new products and services than Neil Anderthal's team. Since both teams are in the R&D business, Wang's team is much "smarter" than Anderthal's team. They create a staggering amount of new knowledge compared to Anderthal's and the other R&D teams.

When we look closely at Josie's team, we see it has a high level of organizational intelligence, and it works differently. It is also led differently. As a result, this team exemplifies what is meant by wisdom workers. And these workers will change everything.

Figure 2.1 shows the team network that is created and leveraged in the metaverse by a wisdom worker leader. The first thing to note is that there is not a hierarchical relationship between the leader and the wisdom workers. Everyone is on the same level. Planning is done cooperatively. Although, not identified in Figure 2.1, some of the members of the team are avatars. One is

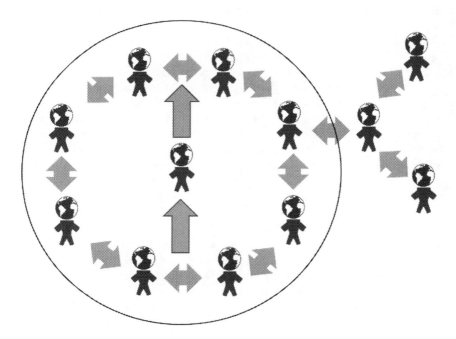

Figure 2.1 Wisdom Worker Network.

notable – Socrates Digital®, who helps facilitate problem-solving sessions with Socratic questioning. These are questions such as "What evidence do you have for the conclusion?," "What concept did you use to analyze the data?," "What assumptions did you use for the data analysis?," "What is your conclusion?," and "What are the implications of your conclusion?."

Socrates Digital® is based off the author's book, Socrates Digital™ for Learning and Problem Solving[1] that describes how to leverage large language models such as ChatGPT for developing a Socratic problem-solving application. It describes how a computer-based Socratic problem-solving system called Socrates Digital® can keep problem-solvers on track, document the outcome of a problem-solving session, and share those results with problem-solvers and larger audiences. In addition, Socrates Digital® assists problem-solvers in combining evidence about their quality of reasoning for individual problem-solving steps and their overall confidence in the solution.

The next thing to notice is that there is no line of control between the leader and the wisdom workers. Team members have control over their projects. That means everyone on the team has an equally important role – leading is just another role. Leading is no more important – or less important – than any of the other roles. However, the big difference between the wisdom worker network and the knowledge worker and manufacturing worker networks is that there are big reciprocal pipelines of knowledge flowing between everyone on the team. (The connecting arrows around the perimeter of the team imply that knowledge pipelines strongly and equally connect everyone.)

In our story, Josie Wang is the leader of the wisdom workers on earth, in the metaverse, and beyond. She is the one in the middle of the team members in Figure 2.1. Luke, the leader of the new Emotional Intelligence Glasses project, is on the right side of the circle of team members. He is connected to a member of another team that will be using the member's network and metaverse to create knowledge for the project. Note that these huge knowledge pipelines cannot exist in the two other networks – the knowledge worker and manufacturing worker. In those networks, the knowledge pipelines would be reduced to trickling information flows or be completely cut off since they would have to flow through the manager.

These huge knowledge pipelines are the secret to the success of Josie Wang's team. As a result of these pipelines, Josie's wisdom workers have increased their capacity to create knowledge – the definition of increased organizational intelligence. In fact, they create three times new knowledge as Neil Anderthal's team. This, of course, results in about three times as much revenue.

There is a new saying in the wisdom economy: "wisdom is money." There are 20 R&D teams in Big Time R&D. Each team spends roughly 1.5 million dollars for expenses and brings in 2 million in revenue. That's 30 million in expenses and 40 million in revenue for the entire company. However, Josie Wang's team brings in 6 million in revenue. If all 20 teams brought in similar revenues, that would be 120 million in revenue – triple the amount of the current level of revenue for the company. As they say, "Individual results may vary." But there's money in those knowledge pipelines. And the leadership of Big Time R&D has noticed.

Instead of trying to increase her control over her team members, thereby reducing knowledge flow, Wang increases the team members' control over their work, which greatly increases knowledge flow. She knows that in the end, it's not what they do that's important – it's the problems they solve that count. And she knows that huge knowledge flows are the result of respect and reciprocity of knowledge between the members of the network – and especially with the leader. They fuel organizational intelligence and the creation of new knowledge.

Josie knows that collaborative leadership is the first key to success for leading in the new wisdom economy. To facilitate collaborative leadership, she uses technology not only in her group meetings to solve problems but also in her communications with her team. Note that her team has 24-hour access to the details of Josie's budget for any project.

Unlike Neil Anderthal, Josie Wang knows her team members' worlds in the metaverse belong to them, and she needs their permission before sharing those worlds with other stakeholders. Like a document library for knowledge workers where they keep drafts of ongoing work, wisdom workers use worlds in the metaverse in various stages of development to capture, manage, and share what they know about a subject. Demanding access to them is akin to demanding access to a team member's private documents, email, and text messages. It invades their privacy. Such a request destroys respect and reciprocity of knowledge between the leader and team members. There will be more on this topic when we look at the heart of the wisdom workers in a later chapter.

Key Actions for Increasing Organizational Intelligence

Employ Collaborative Leadership

- Facilitate Cooperative Planning
- Delegate Control to Team Members
- Instill Reciprocity

Note

1 M. Salisbury, *Socrates Digital™ for Learning and Problem Solving* (Hershey, PA: IGI-Global, 2022).

Chapter 3

Utilize a Problem-Solving Strategy

"I can't stand it any longer," Jake said.

"It's not so bad," Anya said quietly.

"Dr. Anderthal is organized – and he looks good in a suit," Anya mused. "He looks like Cary Grant. Hey! Remember that old movie, 'Topper,' where he plays the part of an angel?"

"Angel?" Jake responded with a frown. "He's the devil!"

"Come on, aren't you going a little too far?" Anya giggled.

"Not at all, "Jake laughed. "Haven't you seen his head spin around?" Then he said as the frown returned, "Anyway, how am I supposed to get these deliverables done? I don't know anybody who's done anything like what he's telling me to do."

Anya tapped her finger on her chin. "Maybe you can send Dr. Anderthal an email and request taking a course at the U – or audit a class to join a professor's research world in the metaverse."

"Well, I suppose I could give it a try," Jake said with a shrug of his shoulders.

At that point, they heard laughter coming from Jared's office next door. They easily recognized Jared's voice as the loud one and heard others in the background who must be on some sort of conference call.

"They seem to be having so much fun – sure wish I could be on that team!" Jake groaned.

Anya let out a sigh as they left the conference room with assignments in hand.

***

"Okay, let's start at the beginning," Josie said. "What is the problem that our client has given us to solve?"

"As I understand it," Luke paused. "Human agents in our intelligence agencies have a hard time assessing the sincerity of the people they converse with in the field. In other words, it's hard to tell if they are being lied to.

DOI: 10.4324/9781003506591-5

Let's consult Socrates Digital® to further define what the problem is. Socrates Digital® can you help us with a problem?"

Certainly, Socrates Digital® replies, "What data, information, or experience do you have?"

"Professor Garrison, at the University of Washington, in his world of emotional intelligence, talks about how hard it is to tell if people are lying to you," Luke said.

Socrates Digital® asked, "Can you give me an example or illustration of your point?"

"In a lecture in his world of emotional intelligence, Professor Garrison, says that even trained professionals are not good at identifying if someone is lying to them," Luke said.

"What assumption underlies this observation?" Socrates Digital® asked.

"People do not want to believe that someone would lie to them," Luke said.

"Do you want to apply this assumption to your reasoning," Socrates Digital® asked.

"Yes," Luke responded.

"Does this assumption hold for the larger data set? How do you know?" Socrates Digital® continued.

Luke pauses and reads the following: "It does hold for the larger dataset. Data gathered from hundreds of cases indicate that agents in the field have, on average, twelve conversations, taking over two hours, and spanning three months to determine if a contact is being truthful with them – and still they are wrong in a third of the cases."

Socrates Digital® responded, "What is the most reasonable conclusion given these concepts, assumptions, and information?"

"Agents in the field have a lot of difficulty in determining if a contact is being truthful with them," Luke replied.

"What are the implications of this conclusion?" Socrates Digital® asked.

"Agents in the field need assistance in determining if a contact is being truthful with them," Luke said.

"Can we get more confirming evidence about this?" Socrates Digital® asked.

"Yes, we can." Luke responded.

Yolanda, this time interacts with Socrates Digital® and examines the information, concepts, and assumptions to come up with a conclusion that a new, small, device is needed to assist agents in determining if a contact is being truthful with them. This conclusion leads to the implication, "A physical device can assist agents in the field in determining if a contact is being truthful with them." After Yolanda tells Socrates Digital® that no other evidence is available currently, Socrates Digital® assists Yolanda in consolidating what is currently known.

"Can we combine this implication with the previous one that states that "Agents in the field need assistance in determining if a contact is being truthful with them?" Socrates Digital® asks.

"Yes," I believe we can," Yolanda said.

Then, can we say that the combined implication is "Agents in the field need a new device to assist them in determining if a contact is being truthful with them?"

"Yes," Yolanda agrees.

"OK," Josie said. We have thought through what the problem is – and have identified a solution. Let's get to work on flushing out the details of that solution by analyzing the information we have, applying appropriate concepts for the analysis, identifying the assumptions we use for the analysis, and determining the conclusions that we make and their associated implications."

After another cup of coffee and some food for thought, Luke worked with the team to lay out a schedule. And finally, "That's a wrap, everyone. Check your watches – that was 85 minutes from idea to plan!"

Josie clapped. "OK – just like always, these results will be in our project world. Don't forget to invite the people to our project world who have dependencies on your work."

"Hey, it's time for lunch," Jared exclaimed.

"So, it is," Josie said as she looked at the time display inside the lens of her glasses. "I have some questions about the moose in the pajamas story," she said with a smile. "See you in the cafeteria!"

***

Problem-Solving Strategy

The problem-solving journey in Josie Wang's team illuminates the art of tapping into organizational intelligence. Their method revolves around collaborative and thorough discourse combined with technological aid. When Jake voices his frustrations, the option to seek outside expertise emerges, underscoring the importance of leveraging external resources and ongoing learning.

However, these wisdom workers show the real crux of their strategy during their session with Socrates Digital®. This AI-driven discourse helps to distill vast and complex data into the components needed for problem-solving: information, assumptions, and concepts. By systematically examining these elements, the team members, including Luke and Yolanda, reach a precise understanding of the problem and a viewpoint of the solution. Notably, this approach ensures that conclusions are logical and supported by credible evidence.

Moreover, the efficiency of these wisdom workers is notable, progressing from problem identification to a detailed plan in just 85 minutes. By inviting stakeholders to their project world, they foster transparency and collaboration. Overall, Josie's team demonstrates a refined, tech-assisted strategy that effectively increases their organizational intelligence, thereby setting the gold standard for problem-solving in the wisdom economy.

Key Actions for Increasing Organizational Intelligence

Utilize a Problem-Solving Strategy

- Identify the Problem to Solve
- Analyze Information, Concepts, and Assumptions to Create Conclusions
- Utilize Implications to Create a Viewpoint for Solving the Problem

Chapter 4

Leverage Artificial Intelligence

Email from Neil Anderthal
  Jake:
  I understand your concern about your assigned deliverable for the new personal transportation device project. However, it seems to me it will only take some good "old fashioned engineering" to get the job done. This is what you were hired to do. I will not authorize any budget for you to take a class or consult with anyone at a university. This is final – DO NOT bring this up again.
  Dr. Neil Anderthal, PhD

***

Next door, Jared's avatar raised his hands exclaiming, "And that's how the moose got into my pajamas!"

  "Okay, we'll have to hear more about that story later," Josie's avatar said with a laugh. "But today, we need to take a detailed look at the feasibility of developing Emotional Intelligence Glasses. If it passes the test, we'll put together a strategy for accomplishing the project."

  Luke's avatar followed up Josie's avatar remarks with, "Since we talked last time, I found some data about 'Informational Glasses.' I worked with Socrates Digital® on measuring biological vital signs, assuming a distance of 100 feet. We ended up with a strong conclusion that it is feasible with the implication that a new device can be developed that measures vital signs at that distance."

  John's avatar added, "I found it very surprising. I didn't realize the data gathering techniques I was familiar with in psychology could be done with physical devices. But, just now, I've been asking questions about the information, concepts to analyze that information, the assumptions used, and the conclusions and implications that follow and found that it does make sense."

DOI: 10.4324/9781003506591-6

Nathan's avatar said, "I was concerned about how to tie a system of different components together. I looked into using some open-source software to develop the firmware for the new device. However, I was worried about the availability of some of the undocumented features in the open-source code. I was able to put those concerns aside by examining some of the information that Jackson collected on the open-source code for a previous project."

"What?" Jackson laughed through his avatar, "Which project was that?!"

Nathan's avatar said. "It was the smart home project. Remember that one?"

"Yeah, given that I have autism, Socrates Digital® gave me a little more guidance and helped me break down the steps for designing and building the smart home project. During the process, I looked up a lot of information in that project world on the features of the open-source software – some of them previously undocumented. Going through the steps with Socrates Digital®, we concluded that the software had the features we need with the implication that it would make a good means for developing the firmware for controlling a smart home – which it did," Jackson's avatar said.

"But it didn't have much on the key features we will need for this project," Nathan's avatar countered. "So, using Socrates Digital®, I went back to your information, and analyzed the information with the assumption, 'analyzing different types of input will improve predictions.' We concluded that the open-source software had the features to process different types of input with the implication it could be successfully used for the Intelligence Glasses project."

"Ooh, I had forgotten most of the reasoning for using the open-source software to develop the firmware for the smart home project – good thing Socrates Digital® didn't forget," Jackson laughed through his avatar. But I think you can gain more confidence in the open-source software as the solution for developing the firmware for the Intelligence Glasses project."

"What do you mean?" Nathan's avatar asked.

"I called call upon Socrates Digital® earlier, Jackson's avatar said. See the discussion log, Socrates Digital® asked if we have more evidence about this solution, I said, 'yes' and offered data that shows that the open-source software can combine evidence from multiple sources. Now, as you see, Socrates Digital® created a new conclusion that the open-source software can combine evidence from multiple sources with the implication that it would make a good means for developing the firmware for combining evidence to improve predictions in the Intelligence Glasses project."

Nathan's avatar shrugged his shoulders. "That's a good addition to my earlier analysis. So, then you have asked Socrates Digital® to help combine the two implications to improve our confidence in using the open-source software for this project?"

"That's right," Jackson's avatar said. "Now, we have a high confidence that the open-source software would make a great – not just good – means for developing the firmware for combining evidence in the Intelligence Glasses project."

"Nice work, guys, it sounds like we have addressed some of the main concerns about completing this project," Josie's avatar said. "Do we now have enough confidence to push forward? Or are there other concerns we need to address?"

After one more issue was discussed, the team decided to move forward with the Emotional Intelligence Glasses project, with Luke as the project lead.

***

Artificial Intelligence

One of the early goals of artificial intelligence was to complete processes or tasks that a human expert has traditionally done. It's easy to see how these wisdom workers extend their mental abilities with artificial intelligence. However, they realize they aim to do something other than replace rational thinking with machine thinking. They practice what Kelly and Hamm described in Smart Machines: "Rather, in the era of cognitive systems, humans and machines will collaborate to produce better results, each bringing their own superior skills to the partnership."[1]

Socrates Digital® is the realization of this partnership. From Jackson's perspective, Socrates Digital® is used to facilitate and improve his problem-solving and help him overcome the decision-making difficulties associated with being on the autism spectrum. From Nathan's perspective, Socrates Digital® provides access to Jackson's previously created solution. However, it is up to Nathan to decide if Jackson's solution applies to a similar problem that Nathan is working on. Ultimately, it is the human, Nathan, in this situation, who can assume responsibility for the consequences of adopting a previous solution – Socrates Digital® cannot take responsibility for this decision.

However, Socrates Digital® can help Nathan decide by asking the right questions to determine if Nathan can successfully adapt the previous solution. For example, Nathan initially consulted with Socrates Digital® to examine the reasoning in concluding that Jackson could use the open-source software to develop the firmware for a smart home project. Afterward, Nathan decided to look into whether he could successfully use the open-source software in the Intelligence Glasses project. Socrates Digital® was there to help Nathan identify the information he would use, the concept he would apply to analyze the information, and the assumptions he would use in that analysis. Next, Socrates Digital® helped Nathan conclude that the open-source software could combine evidence from multiple sources and that he could successfully use the open-source software to develop the firmware for the Intelligence Glasses project.

Key Actions for Increasing Organizational Intelligence

Collaborate with Intelligent Avatars

• Keep Problem-Solving on Track
• Combine Evidence and Determine the Quality of Reasoning
• Capture, Manage, and Distribute Problem-Solving Knowledge

Note

1 J. Kelly and S. Hamm, *Smart Machines: IBM's Watson and the Era of Cognitive Computing* (New York: Columbia University Press, 2013).

Part 2

Organizational Intelligence Requires Courage

Chapter 5

Embrace Opportunities to Lead Others

"Gerald," Dr. Anderthal said. "GERALD," Dr. Anderthal shouted.

Gerald was jarred out of a daydream. "Yes, Dr. Anderthal," he stammered. "What do you want?"

"I want you to pay attention to what's going on in this meeting! As I was saying, Gerald will be taking on the reporting aspect of the new personal transportation device project. The customer is anxious about regular and detailed reporting, so Gerald will make sure we meet those expectations. Please cooperate with him on the reporting needs of this project."

"Do we send our PowerPoint slides to Gerald instead of you?" Jake asked.

"Actually, send them to Dan, the administrative assistant. I'm giving Gerald some of Dan's time to create our project presentations."

Later that week, Jake met up with Anya. "Wow, you look grumpy," she said.

"I just spent the morning redoing my slides for Dr. Anderthal," Jake sighed.

"I thought Gerald was in charge of the PowerPoint slides."

"No, Gerald just makes sure they are in. It's Dan, the admin, who puts them all together."

"So, why did you have to redo them?" Anya asked.

"Anderthal saw my PowerPoint slides on Dan's desk, and he didn't like the way they looked, so he ordered Dan to tell me to redo them all with the new template."

"When did he give out the new template?" Anya asked. "I just saw Gerald and he didn't say anything about a new template."

"I don't think he knows."

"Oh, great," Anya sighed.

***

"I'm pleased with the initial progress on the Emotional Intelligence Glasses project," Luke said. "I was pleasantly surprised, however, with Yolanda's findings on the new sensors that we might be able to use in the glasses."

DOI: 10.4324/9781003506591-8

"Yes, a lot of work has been recently done in the area," Yolanda said. *"I ran onto it by auditing Professor Garrison's class and exploring his world of emotional intelligence at the University of Washington."*

"Then you found his research had been spun out of the University and picked up by a high-tech startup company," Luke added.

"That's right, I found by questioning his digital research assistant, powered by Socrates Digital®, that Professor Garrison's research on emotional intelligence indicators was used to make these new highly sensitive sensors. I described our project to his digital research assistant and asked several questions about them and it answered in the context of our project. The way they work is truly innovative." Yolanda said as she held them up.

"It seems to me that using these new sensors can move the project to another level," Josie said.

"You are right," Luke said. But then he thought for a moment, *"Bringing them out from the lab and into production will be a challenge. It will take more funding. But if we pull it off, it would be the revolutionary product our client is looking for."*

"I believe you are right," Josie said.

"I'm sure the CIA would authorize the additional funding for this. But to be sure, I'll have Ajay Gupta, our Division VP, get the OK from them," Josie said.

Josie turned to the group and looked at Luke. *"Since this would expand the scope of the project significantly, do you think we need to assign a lead to this additional work on the sensors?"*

"I was thinking that same thought," Luke grinned. *"And I have just the person in mind to lead this."*

"Let's hear it," Josie said.

"I think Yolanda would do a great job leading the effort on the new sensors," Luke said.

"I think so, too," Josie said. *"How about it, Yolanda?"*

"Yes," Yolanda responded. *"I would love to head this up, as it's really inspiring what we could do with the new sensors!"*

"I know this is your first time leading an effort, so I can help you with the process," Josie offered with a smile.

"Thanks so much, I can use some help – especially on working with Socrates Digital® to set up a budget and schedule in our project world."

***

Opportunities to Lead Others

The first thing we notice with Anderthal's team is that he is the one who assigns bosses to programs or tasks. Anderthal appointed Gerald to oversee the reporting aspect of the personal transportation project. However, later, Anderthal overrode Gerald's authority by instructing Dan to tell Jake to redo his PowerPoint slides. Not only did he not go through Gerald to get it done, but he also gave orders about the work without informing Gerald. Anderthal provides no opportunities for his team to gain authentic leadership experience.

When team members take leadership positions, they create knowledge about the project that could flow back to the team leader. However, Anderthal does not get back any newly created knowledge about the leadership aspects of his projects. Gerald has nothing to report since Anderthal thinks he already knows what Gerald is doing. As in Figure 2, Anderthal's team has a network with big control lines and small information flow.

On the other hand, in Josie Wang's team, it's a different story. Members of her team do not threaten Josie. She has a high level of confidence in her ability to lead. She is so confident in her abilities that she continually mentors her team members in developing leadership skills. She did not override Luke in his leadership of the Emotional Intelligence Glasses project. She worked collaboratively with Luke to determine if additional oversight was needed to complete the project. After agreeing that Luke needed additional supervision for the newly added sensor aspect, she collaborated with Luke to identify another team member to lead the sensor sub-project. Note that the other team members were also part of this collaboration. They had the opportunity to add input – even to nominate themselves for leading the sensor sub-project.

Josie Wang knows that problem-solving is at the center of all they do. She knows that collaborative leadership – required for leading wisdom workers and elevating organizational intelligence – is a learned set of skills. Josie Wang uses projects as opportunities for team members to learn those leadership skills. As a result, she is growing leaders as they work.

Yolanda embraces the opportunity to lead a sub-project. She is confident in her ability to learn, and she is confident about her other team members. As a result, Yolanda jumps at the chance to learn a new technical area and how to be a better leader. It's all about learning for her, and she sees leading as another skill.

Josie also knows that leadership is a complex skill set. That's why she mentors her team members in leadership skills. Instead of keeping her team under her direct control and having them do simple things, Josie is growing leadership skills in her team that will allow them to successfully take on projects with more complexity. She is intentionally developing her team's leadership capacity, which increases the team's ability to create new knowledge – their organizational intelligence.

Also, Josie knows that technology is vital in being effective as the leader of wisdom workers. She mentors Yolanda in extending her availability to her sub-project team and other stakeholders by working with Socrates Digital® to develop a budget and schedule so that Socrates Digital® can answer questions on a 24/7 basis.

Key Actions for Increasing Organizational Intelligence

Embrace Opportunities to Lead Others

- Exhibit Confidence in Your Ability to Lead
- Provide Opportunities for Others to Learn to Lead
- Mentor Others in Developing Leadership Skills

Chapter 6

Endeavor to Do the Right Thing

"Anya!" She heard his voice. She picked up her pace to turn the corner in the hall. She'll act like she didn't hear him, she thought.

"ANYA!" This time it was a shout.

"Yes, Dr. Anderthal," Anya turned to answer.

He rushed to her. "I just got off the phone with the client for the personal transportation device project. He wants to drop by tomorrow and see how we are doing with it. He's especially interested in what you are working on – the body wrap airbag. I need you to meet with us at 2:00 pm tomorrow."

"I can be there," Anya said.

"Oh, and he heard that you have been working on a preliminary report in your project world about using the body wrap airbag in our project. He wants to see the report before our meeting with him."

"How did he know that I am working on a preliminary report in my private project area about the feasibility of using the body wrap airbag in our project?"

"Just provide a link to the report to me so that I can forward it by 4:00 pm today," Dr. Anderthal said as he turned to walk away.

"But it's not ready for others outside our team," Anya objected.

"Look," he said as he turned back to face her, "this is the time to be a team player. I was asked to create a projected budget for next year by upper management. I have you in the budget right now. There are others who are not yet covered. You don't want to be one of them and get behind on your student loans, do you?"

"I don't have any student loans."

"Okay, your mortgage then."

"I don't have a mortgage, either" Anya said through clenched teeth. "I'll send you the report by the end of the day," she said and turned away towards her office.

DOI: 10.4324/9781003506591-9

"Make it by 4:00. And remember, we are behind on the project, but we don't want him to know that. Use ChapGPT to write the report and make it look like we have made a lot of progress," he shouted over her shoulder.

***

"What's that – carrot cake?" Josie Wang almost jumped out of her chair.

Luke grinned. *"Made it myself. I told you I would bring you something good for our team meeting."*

"I love carrot cake!" Josie cut a big piece and put it on her paper plate. Luke nodded.

"And I like it, too," Jared said as he took the knife from Josie.

"Be sure to try the coffee," Luke said. *"I picked it up from that new coffee place across the street – there's tea, too."*

"Ajay, our VP, said the CIA is excited about the prospect of ramping up the functionality of the glasses," Josie said. *"They will put in the extra funding."*

"Good deal," said Luke. *"I'm not surprised. I gave the project manager at the CIA access to our world for the project. While it's in rough form, it does keep her updated. She can see the progress we are making and the promise of the new sensors for the project."*

"Good move," Josie said as she covered her mouth. *"Now, what needs to be done with the Emotional Intelligence Glasses project?"*

Luke responded, *"We need to do some re-planning given that Yolanda is looking into those new sensors that will transform the project."*

"Sounds like a good idea," Josie said.

"I'll call the project manager at the CIA today and tell her our project will probably slip two months," Luke said. *"After we have re-planned the schedule, I'll update her, so she has the latest information. If I were her, I'd want to know immediately about any changes affecting the projects under my watch."*

"Good," said Josie. *"And, Yolanda, have you talked budget and schedule with that high-tech startup?"*

"Yes," Yolanda said. *"Their ballpark schedule and budget will work for us. I'll be working with them more closely this week to nail it down and bring it to our contract office. And I'll be working with Socrates Digital® to set up a budget and schedule that I'll share with the startup,"* Yolanda said.

"Good," Luke said. *"If we need more time and adjust our schedule, be sure to let the sensor company know in case the schedule slide can help them, too."*

"Don't worry, they will know about it," Yolanda said. "We want them to look out for us if we get into a jam."

***

Do the Right Thing

We can break out having the courage to do the right thing into three categories: personal actions, team-oriented behaviors, and actions on behalf of stakeholders. All three categories involve integrity. All three contribute to the capacity to create knowledge – organizational intelligence.

In the personal category, Neil Anderthal is not doing "the right thing" when he proposes deceiving his client about the progress his team is making on the project. This says a lot about who he is. Such action (if carried out) is a form of lying. Furthermore, claiming work that hasn't been completed is a form of stealing.

In the second category, Anderthal is not endeavoring to do the right thing for the members of his team when he tries to intimidate Anya into deceiving the client about progress on the project. This is wrong for several reasons. For one thing, he is trying to play Anya against her team members for job security. This really damages team dynamics.

In the stakeholder category, Anya quickly recognizes Anderthal's veiled threat about job security. That is, unless she helps to deceive the client about project progress, he will make sure she loses her job.

However, endeavoring to do the right thing is an ingrained value in Josie Wang's team. She does the right thing personally by making sure the client's interests are kept in mind. Note that she might not be the one to watch out for the best interests of the client directly. In the dialogue above, it was Luke who was watching out for the best interests of the client. Yet, Josie is leading even when she is not saying anything outright.

Josie Wang also endeavors to do the right thing by her team members. She does this by making sure they dare to be honest and open with the client about all aspects of the project. This falls under the Golden Rule: "Do unto others what you want them to do to you."[1] Josie endeavors to create a team environment where doing the right thing is the norm and takes priority.

And obviously, Josie's team endeavors to do the right thing for stakeholders, including clients and suppliers. Note how her team has partnered with clients and suppliers on projects. These "outside" team members are kept in the loop about virtually everything on projects. Her team always has the best interests of stakeholders in mind.

Josie also knows technology plays an important role in being able to do the right thing. Socrates Digital® can be used to keep team members and other stakeholders apprised of progress on a multitude of items and events. Socrates Digital® extends the capabilities of these wisdom workers to do the right thing by keeping team members and other stakeholders constantly informed.

Key Actions for Increasing Organizational Intelligence

Endeavor to Do the Right Thing

- Do the Right Thing Yourself
- Do the Right Thing for Your Team
- Do the Right Thing for Your Stakeholders

Note

1 The Golden Rule is found in nearly every religion and culture. It can be seen from many perspectives on human relationships. From a psychological viewpoint, it relates to a person empathizing with others. Philosophically, it involves a person perceiving their neighbor as an extension of his or her self. Sociologically, 'love your neighbor as yourself' is applicable among individuals, groups, and also between individuals and groups.

Chapter 7

Share What Has Been Learned

Anya was 10 minutes early for the meeting.

"Hi, there! I'm Mark Salazar with Big Automotive," he said.

"Hi, I'm Anya."

"Tanya?"

"No, it's like leaving the 'T' off of Tanya. It's Russian."

"Wow," Mark said. "My daughter is expecting a baby girl. I'm going to tell her about your name! It's short, easy to pronounce, and has a nice ring to it."

Anya blushed a little. "Thanks, glad you like it."

Dr. Anderthal glided in. "I see you have met Anya. We can get started."

As Dr. Anderthal started going through the presentation, Anya recognized the slides of her team members. Apparently, he had "repackaged" their slides into his presentation. She also noted there was no indication of her contribution or anyone else's.

"Now, that's what I'm interested in," said Mark. Anya looked up to see one of her slides. It was the first slide of several on the body wrap airbag.

"Dr. Anderthal, I used ChatGPT to generate a summary of your preliminary report. In my summary, it said that the body wrap airbag will protect a human being from serious injury up to 100 miles-per-hour," Mark said.

"That's right," Dr. Anderthal responded.

"Well, that's not exactly correct at this time," Anya said quietly.

"What do you mean?" Mark asked. "I saw in my summary report last night that it will protect a human being from serious injury up to 100 miles-per-hour."

"Well," Anya responded. "I'm still working on that 100-mph answer. ChatGPT sometimes misreports some facts. In this case, the preliminary report is currently based on projections from a new prototype airbag that hasn't been tested yet."

"At present, what is the maximum speed that a human could escape injury from an accident on a personal transportation device?" Mark asked.

DOI: 10.4324/9781003506591-10

"80 miles-per-hour," Anya said. *"They are tested and certified for that speed. However, there is a lot of confidence that the new airbags will perform satisfactorily at 100 mph. But there isn't any real data yet to support that claim."*

Mark turned to Dr. Anderthal. *"It looks like she knows more about your project than you do!"*

Dr. Anderthal's face turned red, and he stared at Anya.

"Well, I was excited about the 100mph airbag," Mark said. *"We have a big opportunity for marketing a personal transportation device to the Europeans, and there are several countries where people are going 100 mph."*

"We'll keep you updated on the new airbag," Dr. Anderthal said.

"Okay, thanks," Mark said as he picked up his coat. *"Nice meeting you, Anya. Who knows, I may have a little Anya in my life soon."*

"Nice meeting you," Anya said.

After the door closed, Dr. Anderthal stared at Anya. *"Next time, you give me something to share, make sure it has the right answers in it!"*

Anya stared at the floor until he left.

Dr. Anderthal went to his office. A moment later, he heard a knock at the door.

"Who is it?" he snorted.

"Gerald," the response came in a barely audible voice.

"Come in and sit down. I have an assignment for you," Dr. Anderthal said. He went on to explain what he wanted Gerald to do.

"You want me to spy on Wang's team?"

"NO! Think of it as early reporting – something that can help the company become more nimble. Now, get to it!"

Gerald stumbled out into the hall. No one heard him say, *"Sounds like spying to me."*

Meanwhile, just down the hall, Anya told Jake what happened to her with Dr. Anderthal.

"That's what he said to you? That's some 'thank you'! What a jerk!"

"Well, in a sense he was right," Anya said. *"I didn't make sure all the answers were accurate and complete."*

"How come?" Jake responded as he began to calm down.

"Yesterday around noon, he told me he wanted my preliminary report updated by four o'clock. I didn't want to share it like it was. I have other work in the report, too. And…"

"And what?" Jake asked, now getting curious.

"I knew that he would take credit for all my work, so I left in only the stuff that related to the airbags for the personal transportation project. I didn't want him later taking credit for the other problems that I've worked hard to solve."

"And the report didn't look positive for the airbags to function at 100 miles per hour?" Jake responded.

"That's right," Anya whispered.

"Serves him right," Jake said.

***

"Hi, everyone," Luke's avatar said. "In case you have forgotten, this is Heather Wilton of the CIA. She's the manager of the Emotional Intelligence Glasses project."

"Good to see you, again," Josie Wang's avatar said.

"Good to be here," Heather's avatar responded with a smile.

"I know Heather has a plane to catch, so I thought we could give her a quick overview of our progress," Luke's avatar said.

"I think I have a pretty good idea of where things are," Heather's avatar said. "Luke has kept me updated on the project with weekly reports – which I really appreciate. How about if I ask Socrates Digital® some questions about the project?"

"Sure, go right ahead," Luke's avatar said.

"Then let's go right to this new development with the sensors," Heather's avatar said. "Socrates Digital® what can you tell me about the sensor technology described in the project?"

Socrates Digital® responded "This new break-through sensor technology will allow picking up the heartbeat, blood pressure, and skin moisture at a distance as described in this white paper."

"I'm curious about how that will work," Heather's avatar said.

"Well, let's have Yolanda speak to this," Luke's avatar responded. "Those are her initials on the bottom of the preliminary report that Socrates Digital® pulled up. She's the expert on the sensors."

"Yes, it is possible to pick up vital signs from a human being at a distance," Yolanda's avatar said.

"The white paper that Socrates Digital® pulled up says it can be done from a distance of 100 feet," Heather's avatar said.

"That's correct," Yolanda's avatar said, "as long as there are not any adverse weather conditions such as a hailstorm."

"So, it's a straight-forward process to feed these vital signs into an application that can tell if someone is lying?" Heather's avatar asked.

"That's right," Yolanda's avatar said. "And we predict the accuracy will be quite good when combined with data on the gestures of the human subject."

"So that feature can be developed from what is known in the area of informational glasses?" Heather's avatar asked.

"That's right," Luke's avatar said. "We worked with Socrates Digital® to determine if we can have confidence in combining discoveries from different fields to create a new and innovative device with never-before-seen capabilities. Socrates Digital® identified the knowledge about gestures from the area

of informational glasses and helped us combine it with knowledge about vital signs."

"So, not yet demonstrated, but a proposed solution in which you have high confidence that an operative could wear the glasses, and it would automatically recognize the speaker, display what is known about the speaker on the inside lens of the glasses and indicate if the speaker is telling the truth," Heather's avatar said.

"Yes, and the trick is putting all this together into a set of glasses," Luke's avatar said. "Jared is looking into the software that will tie it all together. I think that catches you up on the project."

"Thanks – I feel that I am" Heather's avatar said. "One question, though. Can I get access to the technical requirements and testing data for the new sensors?"

"I'm working on that," Yolanda said. "As you know, Socrates Digital® answers questions on the capabilities of the sensors based on what we have discovered, but it's pretty general. The small startup company that will develop the sensors has not released any reports on the performance of the sensors. After they have released their report to us, you can ask Socrates Digital® any questions about the report at that time."

"Thank you, I'll look for it," Heather's avatar said.

"Anything else we can provide you at this time?" Luke's avatar asked.

"No, that should do it, and now I'm off to catch my plane," Heather's avatar said. "Oh, but there's one last comment. I want you to know how much I appreciate how you keep me in the loop on this project. It's great always to know the status. I wish all my projects were like this one! I'll keep you updated on any changes on my end."

***

Share Knowledge

It's clear now that Neil Anderthal doesn't share knowledge with others. Note that while he tells Anya to be at the meeting with their client, Mark Salazar, Anya does not know what Anderthal has told him. If experience predicts her role in the meeting, she will only be there if Anderthal gets into trouble.

And get into trouble, he does. First of all, he presents the team's work as his own. The client probably thinks Anderthal did only some of the work himself, even though he may have directed it. What becomes disturbing to Salazar is when Anderthal doesn't know the answer to one of his questions.

In trying to do the right thing for the client, Anya speaks up and reveals a discrepancy in Anderthal's response to Salazar's question. Anya's correction directly results from Anderthal's pattern of not giving credit to other people's work. He had given the impression that the report created by Anya was something he had created himself. By not crediting Anya for her work and not referring Salazar's question to her, Anderthal very likely lost some respect from the client and possibly the client's confidence in the project.

Think back to the Manufacturing Worker Network depicted in Figure 1.2. Remember the big control lines and the small information flow returning to the boss? Anya's behavior explains why the information flowing back to Anderthal is so tiny. Anya doesn't trust him because he doesn't share what he knows or give credit to others for their work. As a result, she goes out of her way to limit what she shares with him. That's right. Instead of going out of her way to share helpful information with him, she deliberately limits what she shares. We are witnessing the principle of negative reciprocity in this situation.

Neil Anderthal probably knows Anya is holding back. He still needs to see how to create value in the wisdom economy. Anderthal thinks his team produces value by getting things done. He must appreciate that new knowledge is the most exceptional value his team creates for his clients. Thus, while his team is creating new knowledge while completing projects, he doesn't see any of it – and no one else does either, for that matter.

We don't hear much from Josie Wang during her team meeting with an important client. But she has already done her preliminary work for the meeting. She places credit and responsibility where they belong. Luke oversees the Emotional Intelligence Glasses project for the CIA. He contacts the client, Heather Wilton, and invites her to his virtual meeting. Josie is there in support if the client raises broader questions about managing the project.

Luke also follows Josie's lead in placing credit and responsibility where they belong for the project. When asked a question by Wilton, Luke refers the question to Yolanda. Clearly, Yolanda gets the credit for the knowledge she has created for the project and is responsible for providing the most informed and accurate response to the client.

Yolanda shared what she had learned with her team members during the project. Yolanda has also shared with the client during the project's life by providing the client access to Socrates Digital®. In addition, Yolanda shares with the startup company that will manufacture the sensors. And they share with her. It's an example of the principle of positive reciprocity at work here.

Josie's team also uses technology to credit individual team members for creating and sharing knowledge. For example, when Heather Wilton asked Socrates Digital® about different aspects of the project, she received more than just answers. She also learned about the source of the information she obtained. Wilton knew that answers to her questions about the sensor came from Yolanda. Similarly, she realized that explanations about the possibility of using human gestures to improve the performance of the glasses came from a report created by Luke.

In Figure 7.1, the medal symbolizes that wisdom workers dare to embrace opportunities to lead others, endeavor to do the right thing, and share what they have learned.[1]

Figure 7.1 The Courage of the Wisdom Worker.

Key Actions for Increasing Organizational Intelligence

Share What You Have Learned

- Share Knowledge
- Give Credit for Others' Work
- Use Sharing to Instill Reciprocity

Note

1 Yep, the medal does smack of the Wizard of Oz. However, the Wizard was right in that it is still the best way to depict the presence of courage.

Part 3

Organizational Intelligence Requires Heart

Chapter 8

Convey Personal Integrity

"Hey, where did you get those funny glasses?" Anya asked with a laugh.

*"Yolanda, from Josie's team, is letting me play with them for an hour,"
Jake said. "They are Alpha Alpha – she just taped the parts together."*

"What do they do?"

"Let's find out."

Anya frowned.

"Do you like your boss?" Jake asked.

"What kind of question is that?" Anya replied, obviously annoyed.

"Just play along with me," Jake said.

"Okay," and after a pause, "Yes, I like my boss."

"Wow!" Jake said. "This thing really does work!"

"What?"

"It really works," Jake repeated.

Anya looked baffled.

"It detected that you were lying," Jake said.

"No way," Anya said as she pulled closer and looked at the glasses.

*"See," Jake said as he pulled off the glasses and turned the inner lens
toward her. "Here is your face. And here is the confidence level displayed in
red showing that you were lying – 88%!"*

"That's amazing," she said.

"Hey, you two better get to the meeting or you'll be late," Gerald said.

Jake and Anya hurried to the conference room.

"You're late," said Dr. Anderthal.

"Sorry," they said in one voice.

*"Okay – let's get this meeting started," Dr. Anderthal said. "This slide
shows our budget to date for the personal transportation device project."*

"Uhhhhhh," stammered Gerald.

"What's the matter?" Dr. Anderthal asked.

*"I think I turned in a smaller number for the total hours we have charged,"
Gerald said quietly.*

"No, this is what you turned in."

DOI: 10.4324/9781003506591-12

"I don't think so."

"THIS IS WHAT YOU TURNED IN, AND THAT'S FINAL," shouted *Dr. Anderthal. And he looked right at Gerald. "And don't tell anyone anything different."*

Jake gasped and jumped up.

"What do you want?" Dr. Anderthal asked. "And why are you wearing those ridiculous glasses?"

"Eye strain," gasped Jake. "Gotta go, I think I'm going to get sick."

Anya caught up with Jake after the meeting. "Why did you rush out like that," she said.

"He's lying about the budget," Jake said quietly.

"How do you know?"

Jake took off the glasses and turned the inner lens toward her. She saw Anderthal's face. Over it, she saw the confidence level displayed in red. It read 94%.

***

"Hey, are those cinnamon rolls?" It was a voice from the hallway.

"You bet," Yolanda said as she put down the big pan. "Gerald, you are welcome to have one."

"I'm in," Gerald said as he picked up one and put it on a small plate.

"And you are welcome to some coffee," Yolanda said. "I got it at the place across the street that Luke likes so much."

"Mmmm, looks good. Thanks, Yolanda," Josie said as she picked up her roll.

"And I've got mine, so let's start this team meeting," said Luke.

"I've got some bad news, so maybe I should go first," said Jared.

"Okay," said Luke. "I bet it's about the open-source software."

"Yep," said Jared. "I thought I could use the undocumented features to tie all the components together."

"Well, it seems to work, as we have taped together a prototype," Yolanda said.

"Yeah, it works for a while, but then it seems to time out and locks up," said Jared. "I've spent a lot of time on it, and I just can't get those undocumented features to work consistently."

"So, what's the solution?" Luke asked.

"We'll have to write some new code for the open-source software to provide the functionality of the undocumented features," said Jared.

"And the time and budget for that?" asked Luke.

"2 guys for 6 months – or 1 year FTE,"

"Ouch," said Josie.

"Yeah, sorry," said Jared. "That's why I put so much effort trying to use the undocumented features so we could avoid the cost and delay. But I just couldn't get them to work as we need them to work."

"It happens," Luke said. He turned to Josie. "I don't think we can pass this on to the client, can we?"

"No, we can't," said Josie. "We will probably have to eat it."

"Well, it's the right thing to do," said Luke. "And this client really does appreciate our ethics around things like this."

"Indeed," said Josie. "And you have to take the long view on situations like this. Having integrity will let you sleep at night and get you more business in the future." She put on a little smile.

Gerald got up, signaling a 'thank you' to Yolanda, and shuffled out of the room.

"Wait a second" Jared exclaimed. "This looks promising!"

"What is it? Luke asked.

"I posted a request for help on several developer community boards. "I did this a few days ago and thought I came up empty. But just now, one of the community members sent me a link to his Socrates Digital®. He said that a friend of mine said that I would repay him someday. And, after asking it a couple of questions, it looks like I have access to the information that I need about those undocumented features."

"So, you used your good name to gain access to a person's Socrates Digital® who you didn't even know?" Luke asked.

"It pays to keep your cred up," Jared said with a smile.

***

Personal Integrity

By using the new Emotional Intelligence Glasses, Jake had evidence that Dr. Anderthal wasn't telling the truth about the numbers on the presentation slide he received from Gerald. Not only had Dr. Anderthal lied about the numbers on the slide, but he also tried to intimidate Gerald and the others into accepting his lie. And this lie had another aspect of dishonesty about it: lying about the number of hours he planned to charge the client for work they hadn't done. Again, this is a form of stealing. Finally, Dr. Anderthal isn't concerned with these dishonest acts; he is more concerned with his reputation and uses intimidation to cover up his dishonesty.

Josie Wang's team works in a completely different manner. She creates a culture where the truth is preferred and always expected. When the team learned they had taken a dead end by relying on undocumented features to provide the needed functionality in the open-source software, they realized it would cost them, not their client, to make it right. In the end, they were committed to the notion of "giving a day's work for a day's pay." This commitment means they would not bill the client for work unrelated to the project. Josie's comments and actions reinforce the value that they, as individuals and as a team, should be more concerned about integrity than short-term losses on a project.

But the story takes a turn when Jared uses technology to search to find the solution to his problem. However, it turns out that technology has only extended Jared's reach. His "good name" still gives him access to the solution.

Key Actions for Increasing Organizational Intelligence

Convey Personal Integrity

- Tell the Truth
- Give a Day's Work for a Day's Pay
- Maintain Personal Integrity

Chapter 9

Believe in Something Larger than Yourself

"What's that?" Dr. Anderthal asked.

"Girl Scout Cookies," Anya said. "I'm selling them for my nieces."

"This isn't the place for that kind of thing. Put them away."

Anya put the cookies on a chair in the back of the room and placed her coat over them.

"Now, let's get down to business," Dr. Anderthal said.

"Gerald, give us a report on the schedule and budget for the personal transportation device project," said Dr. Anderthal.

"Well, uh, it looks like we are on budget and schedule," Gerald responded.

"But we only have six weeks to go," interrupted Dr. Anderthal. "And we are not even close to delivering a prototype for the client."

The room was silent for a few moments.

Dr. Anderthal put his hands on his waist and straightened up. "We are behind on this project. We need to pull together as a team to get the job done. We will have to work the next couple of weekends to get back into the game."

A groan arose throughout the room.

"Oh, come on, we should all be able to put in some extra work for the team," Dr. Anderthal said. He looked at Jake. "Is there a reason you can't work on this during the next couple of weekends?"

Jake nodded and sighed. "I was planning on working on the new kitchen for the homeless teen center."

"Well, this is more important than that for the next two weekends. This is your job, for crying out loud! We only work 32 hours during the week. In the old days, we worked 60 hours a week. No one knows how to work anymore!" With that, Dr. Anderthal picked up his things and left the room.

"Other things are important, too," Jake said softly. "Work isn't everything."

***

"Girl Scout cookies?" Josie Wang asked.

"You bet!" John said. "That plate is free – please help yourself. And the packages are for sale. I'm selling them for my daughter."

DOI: 10.4324/9781003506591-13

"I love their thin mints," said Josie with a smile.

"Me, too," said Jared as he scooped up a handful.

"What's this?" Josie asked as she held up a paper flyer.

"That's a reminder about the volunteer project we decided to do as a group this year," Yolanda said. "As a company-sponsored volunteer project, we will meet this Friday at the homeless teen center to put in a new kitchen for them."

"I'll bring my hammer," Josie said.

"And remember that some of us will be volunteering our own time over the next couple of weekends to finish it up," Yolanda said. "So, you are all welcome to join the effort."

"It's a good cause," Josie said. "That teen shelter can sure use a new kitchen."

"All good," said Luke. "Now let's turn our attention to the Emotional Intelligence Glasses project."

"According to your slide, it looks like we are back on schedule and budget," Josie said before taking a bite out of her cookie.

"We are indeed, thanks to Jared for pulling our bacon out of the fire," Luke said as he handed Jared a thin mint. "Here's the team award for bacon-saving!"

"Thanks – and the preliminary tests show that the fix I found is doing the trick," Jared said. "We now have a reliable system up and running!"

Yolanda added, "And we now have some early findings showing that the glasses actually work in a field setting!"

"Hooray!" said Josie as high fives went around the room. Don't forget, please use ChatGPT to update your reports with the new findings and make them accessible to Socrates Digital® before Friday. With Socrates Digital® on the job, we won't be missed while working on the new kitchen for the homeless teen shelter."

"Good, so let's look at what we need to do to bring the Emotional Intelligence Glasses project in for a landing," said Luke.

***

Something Larger than Yourself

It's clear what Neil Anderthal believes in. He believes in himself and puts his energy into getting ahead. As far as he is concerned, there is no greater cause than working to put himself in a better position. In this chapter, Anderthal tells his team that getting the project done on time is the top priority. Although he doesn't realize it, his team is in the knowledge creation business. However, Anderthal's strong lines of control have stifled the creation of new knowledge. So now, he finds his team is behind schedule. Unfortunately, his response is to strengthen his lines of control to get the job done. Since the strong lines of authority have yet to work to keep the project on track, he is cracking down on his team to bring the project on schedule. It's the only thing that matters to him, and he has taken to intimidation to make it the only thing that matters to his team.

On the contrary, Josie Wang's team members believe in something larger than themselves. At the same time, they don't all share the same religious or spiritual beliefs. They all believe in their organization and the need to help others. This belief is shown in a small way by the Girl Scout cookies John brought to the meeting. It's shown in a greater way by how the whole team gets behind building a new kitchen for the homeless teen center. Some team members even planned to contribute their weekend time to finish building the kitchen. We are not told, although we sense it, that this team performs many other volunteer activities outside of work. Such volunteerism is fundamental to their values and belief in something larger than themselves.

This characteristic is not lost on Big Time R&D leadership. In response to such employees, they have sponsored a community volunteer day. For the members of Josie's team, this means working for an organization that believes in something larger than the organization. And that is even more important to Josie's team members than those at the top of Big Time R&D currently realize. That's because these team members align their personal goals with something larger than themselves. It's critically important to them. And Josie Wang knows it.

Key Actions for Increasing Organizational Intelligence

Believe in Something Larger than Yourself

- Believe in Something Larger than Your Team
- Believe in Something Larger than the Organization
- Align Personal Goals with Something Larger than Yourself

Chapter 10

Take on Best Interests of Those You Lead

"So, are you sure they will be way over budget and schedule?" Dr. Anderthal asked.

"Yes, I was there," Gerald said.

"It hasn't appeared in her monthly report. So, Josie is trying to hide it until after they name the new VP to replace Ajay?" Dr. Anderthal stroked his chin. "Okay, I'm off!"

"Good luck!" Gerald said and walked down the hall toward his office.

Jake and Anya peaked around the corner. They looked at each other wondering if they had really heard what they thought they heard.

Dr. Anderthal strode to Ajay's office. He paused outside, took a deep breath, and knocked on the door.

"Come in," said a distracted voice.

"Hi Ajay," Dr. Anderthal said.

"Oh, it's you," said Ajay Gupta, the Division VP for Big Time R & D. "Come on in. What can I do for you?"

"I'm afraid I have some disturbing news."

"And what is that?" as he looked up and turned to Dr. Anderthal.

"New glasses?" Dr. Anderthal asked.

"Well, sort of – this is the new prototype that Josie Wang's team is working on," Ajay said. "Now, what is this about?"

"Well," Dr. Anderthal said, "I don't like going to my supervisor about another team leader, but there are a lot of problems with that project."

"What kind of problems?"

"They are way behind schedule and way over budget."

"Funny, that's not what the monthly report says," said Ajay. "And Josie never said anything about it. How did you find out?"

"Well, umm, the client told me," Dr. Anderthal said.

"Heather Wilton, of the CIA?" Ajay asked.

Dr. Anderthal nodded his head.

"I see," said Ajay. "You know we are looking to replace me with a new VP when I become CEO. And you know that you and Josie are both being considered."

DOI: 10.4324/9781003506591-14

"I know," said Dr. Anderthal. "I wouldn't bring it up since it could hurt Josie's chances for the job, but it's such an important contract that I wouldn't feel right about it unless I brought my concerns to you."

"Okay, I think I get the picture. I'll look into it and take some corrective action."

"Thanks. Sorry to have to bring this to your attention."

"It's okay," Ajay said. "I believe things happen for a reason."

Dr. Anderthal quietly closed the door behind him. Once in the hall, he smiled to himself.

Ajay scratched his head, took off the glasses, and put them on his desk. He let out a heavy sigh. Anderthal's image was on the inside lens of the glasses. It displayed 98% in red for the confidence level. He was lying.

***

Josie Wang looked up when she heard a knock on her door.

"Come in," she said.

Jake opened the door and followed Anya in.

"Good to see you." said Josie. "Would you like a Girl Scout Cookie?"

"Sure, I love thin mints," Jake said as he took one.

"I'm okay," Anya said as she waved off the cookies.

"What brings you two to my office?" Josie asked.

"Well, it's delicate," Jake said.

"Okay, so, fire away," Josie said with a smile.

"We think our boss might be trying to hurt you," Jake said. Then Jake and Anya told Josie what they heard in the hall and seeing Dr. Anderthal go immediately to Ajay's office.

"What time did this happen?" Josie asked.

"Around 2:00," said Anya.

"Well, let me check something," said Josie. She quickly pulled up Socrates Digital® and looked at the last conversation about budget and schedule for the project.

"No worries," Josie said. "I checked my log for Socrates Digital® on budget and schedule and saw that Ajay asked some questions. And it was 2:13 this afternoon. It answered his question by telling him we are on budget and schedule. I'm sure he saw Heather's comments after her questions the day before. She gave us a lot of praise for our work."

"So, it was Gerald that told Neil," Josie said. She thought for a moment. "I remember Gerald being at our meeting for a few minutes the other day."

"But you shouldn't hold it against Gerald," Jake said.

"How come?" Josie asked.

"I'm sure he was bullied into doing it by Dr. Anderthal," Jake said.

"Well, no harm was done," Josie said. "My leader is happy and so is my client."

"Gosh, you have a great attitude, Josie. I would've been mad," said Jake. "How do you do it?"

"I'm disappointed, but not mad," she said. "I try to live my life honestly and transparently. When Ajay and Heather ask Socrates Digital® a question about my budget and schedule, they – in a sense – ask me that question. Since they know me, they know that the answer they get from Socrates Digital® is truthful. This gives me a lot of confidence that I am keeping people updated about what is happening with our work. So, I don't worry when things like this come up."

"But he lied about you," Anya said.

"Well, perhaps, he didn't think he was," Josie said. "I remember the discussion when Gerald dropped in. We were discussing a problem that would drive the project over budget and schedule. I think Gerald left before we found a solution to the problem. It's almost a little bit funny."

"Well, it's not funny to us," Anya said quietly. "He bullies us to do unethical things, too."

The smile left Josie's face. *"It sounds like you need to talk to Ajay about this. All you need to do is ask for a skip level meeting."*

"Let us tell you the other things he is doing," Jake said.

Josie held her finger up. *"I shouldn't hear this," she said. "Take this all to Ajay. That's the right way to do this."*

"I suppose you are right," Jake said. "It's the right thing for Dr. Anderthal if we don't gossip about him. But why are you protecting him?"

"It's the right thing to do for all of us," said Josie. "We don't want to gossip about people. We want to discuss any problems we have with the person who can fix the problems. For you, that's Ajay."

"Okay, for the good of the organization, we will talk to Ajay," Jake said with a sigh.

"And it's the right thing for you, too," Josie said with a smile.

"Why is that important?" Jake asked.

"Because it's my job to make it as easy as possible for you to do the right thing," Josie said.

"Even if we don't work for you?" Anya asked.

"Even if you don't work WITH me," Josie said with a smile.

***

Best Interests of Those You Lead

Neil Anderthal did not take on the best interests of his team members. He did just the opposite. He made Gerald take on his personal best interests. Anderthal forced Gerald to put aside his work for the company and spy on another team. All so Anderthal could get information to use to improve his chances for a promotion. Anderthal was coopting Gerald's time – paid for by the company – to work on his personal goals. Refocusing Gerald to work on Antherthal's personal vendetta is not only a case of bullying an employee, but it is also a case of stealing. When Gerald is doing Anderthal's personal bidding, they are both stealing from the company since Gerald should be attending to company work. Anderthal is the biggest offender of this crime because he uses his authority to direct another person in this unethical activity.

However, the actual costs don't stop there. Anderthal's actions after the spying incident are potentially costly to the company. He is attempting to damage the reputation of one of the company's top performers – Josie Wang. In a strongly networked world of work, this could lower the trust team members and stakeholders have in Josie and reduce the flow of knowledge her team creates. As we discussed before, this will decrease the revenue her team brings in, thus hurting the best interests of the company. But that does not bother Anderthal. He is only concerned about pursuing his own best interests.

Josie Wang, however, takes on the best interests of those she leads. In doing so, she takes on the best interests of her team members. As seen in the many dialogues preceding the one in this chapter, Josie has repeatedly looked after the best interests of her team members. In this chapter, she also looks after the best interests of Anderthal's team members. Josie creates a space for Jake and Anya to do the right thing. And Josie guides them to do the right thing for themselves, their leader, and the organization. She sums it up by noting that for them to do the right thing for others is ultimately the right thing for them as well. Josie truly knows these wisdom workers.

Google did an extensive search to determine the characteristics of successful teams. The findings revealed the overall factor in successful teams was a high level of psychological safety. In other words, they could tell their teammates the most intimate things about their lives. Josie creates a culture of psychological safety for her team members (e.g., John sharing about his wife's illness in Chapter 1) and similarly in this chapter for Jake and Anya. A good summary of this study can be found in The New York Times Magazine.[1]

Josie took on her organization's best interests when she ensured Anderthal's actions did not harm the organization. Josie was also looking after Ajay's best interests when she did this. She knew he would be concerned about Anderthal's disclosure, so she ensured he accessed the answers he needed from Socrates Digital® to feel confident the project was on track.

Josie showed she also takes on the best interests of her stakeholders when she looked at the log for Socrates Digital® to see if her client had concerns with the project. She wanted to ensure Heather Wilton didn't get any unnecessary heartburn over Anderthal's actions.

Note that Socrates Digital® becomes a tool Josie can use to take on the best interests of others. When Josie is in meetings – or even not at work – her team members can tap into Josie's expertise by asking questions of Socrates Digital®.

Figure 10.1 The Heart of the Wisdom Worker.

The same is true for others in her organization – such as her supervisor, Ajay. And it's true for her outside stakeholders – such as her CIA project manager, Heather Wilton.

In Figure 10.1, we see that wisdom workers have the heart to convey personal integrity, believe in something larger than themselves, and take on the best interests of those they lead.[2]

Key Actions for Increasing Organizational Intelligence

Take on the Best Interests of Those You Lead

- Take on the Best Interests of Team Members
- Take on the Best Interests of the Organization
- Take on the Best Interests of Project Stakeholders

Notes

1 C. Duhigg, What Google Learned From Its Quest to Build the Perfect Team. *The New York Times Magazine*, February 25, 2016.
2 More wisdom from the Wizard of Oz. This shape is still the best way to depict the presence of heart.

Part 4

Organizational Intelligence Requires Leadership

Chapter 11

Grow Their Brains

"Did you hear about Jake and Anya?" Jim blurted out.

"No, what's up with them?" Jackie wondered.

"Something went wrong with the personal transportation project, and they are now in Josie Wang's group!" Jim said.

"What?" Jackie groaned. "Lucky dogs! Hey, if it takes tanking a project to get out of this group, I'm all for it."

"Let's get to it," Dr. Anderthal said as the door swung shut behind him.

"Where are Jake and Anya?" Jackie asked.

Dr. Anderthal stared at Jackie for a moment. "The funding for the personal transportation device project was discontinued. They were reassigned to Josie Wang's team. That team is short-handed."

"But we need them here," Jackie said. "We have two other projects coming to a close, and we still need to do all the reporting."

"Well, we'll make do," said Dr. Anderthal. "We might have to work some weekends to get those reports completed. Now, let's see where we are on those projects."

Heavy sighs were drowned out by the sound of binders opening.

***

"Welcome, Jake and Anya, to our team," Josie said.

"It's good to be here," Jake said with a smile.

"Likewise," Anya said, catching Jake's smile.

"I hope you don't mind. I invited Ajay to our onboarding meetings," Josie said.

Jake and Anya looked puzzled.

"Josie's team is the most productive R & D team in our company – maybe, the world!" said Ajay with a smile. "I asked Josie if I could sit in on her new team members' meetings so I could see how she does it."

Jake and Anya nodded.

DOI: 10.4324/9781003506591-16

"You said we would have a two-hour meeting every week for the next three weeks?" Jake asked. "How come so much time to get onboard? Do you have secret handshakes or something?"

Josie smiled. "In a way we do," she said. "You will find we are very purposeful here. We share the same values for ourselves, our team members, and our stakeholders. Above all, everyone strives to make our team a place with a high level of psychological safety."

Jake and Anya looked puzzled.

Josie let out a little laugh. "That means you can say anything that you want, and no one will judge you for it. All ideas, beliefs, and hunches are welcome here."

"Now, let's get to this week's topics," she said. "Let's start by talking about how we work here."

Jake and Anya looked at each other.

"We use a collaborative leadership model," Josie said. "I'm responsible for facilitating cooperative planning for our projects."

"That means the whole team works together to plan a project?" Jake wondered.

"That's right," Josie said. "We want more than just my brain working on the planning. We engage the whole team in reducing the chance we haven't thought of something important."

"Makes sense," Anya said.

"After the project is planned, the control or leadership for the project belongs to the team. The team selects a team leader for that project."

"You pick the leader?" Jake asked.

"I have input, but the team picks the leader," Jose said. "Usually, someone steps up to be the leader because they have the most technical knowledge in the area. Or better said, they have the most potential for solving the problems needed to complete the project successfully," Josie said with a smile.

"Then, what do you do?" Jake asked.

"Good question!" Josie said. "I make sure we employ collaborative leadership, so each team member has the most control over his or her part of the project. This allows team members the most flexibility for engaging in problem-solving to successfully complete the project."

Josie paused a moment before continuing. "It also means they have the responsibility for successfully completing the project in their own hands."

Ajay leaned forward in his chair as if he had just had an "Ah Ha" moment.

"You talk a lot about problem-solving," Anya said. "Why is it so important?"

"Most people still think that you get paid for the work you do," Josie said. "On this team, we believe you get paid for the new knowledge you create. So, we really focus on problem-solving."

Jake and Anya looked at each other.

"Machines can now do just about everything we can describe," Josie said. *"It takes a person to solve a problem and share that knowledge with someone else so it can be applied to a new and different problem. That's how the wisdom workers create value for their organizations."*

Anya scratched her head. *"Okay,"* she said. *"I get that the real value we bring as workers is the new knowledge we create. But why do we need to change the way we manage projects?"*

"Well, think of it this way," Josie said. *"As your leader, I can make you do things. But I can't make you think – or solve a problem. So, I need to give you all the room that I can so you can solve the problems that lead to successfully completing the project."*

"Okay, now that makes sense," Anya said.

Jake inserted, *"Hey, I've noticed you use a lot of smart technology in your group. That must make it fun to work here!"*

"Yes, it does, but it's not the reason we use technology so much," Josie responded with a smile. *"Since knowledge creation is our business, we use technology to make us smarter so we can solve problems faster and better..."*

"To create new knowledge," Jake said. *"Sorry to interrupt."*

"It's okay. Remember, this is a safe place," Josie said with a nod of approval. *"We use technology to extend our cognitive abilities to reason about data and information, make conclusions, and use the implications to develop solutions for the problems that stand in our way."*

"Artificial Intelligence!" Jake said.

"That's right, we use artificial intelligence to enhance our cognitive abilities for making better decisions," Josie nodded.

"Gives you bigger brains!" Jake exclaimed.

Anya gave him a *"that's enough"* look.

Jake nodded sheepishly.

Josie smiled. *"Remember that while a machine may provide the information and reasoning we need to make good decisions, we take responsibility for the decisions that are made – not the machine."*

"How does using a problem-solving strategy come in?" Anya asked.

"Since we see knowledge creation as our product, we see problem-solving as the way to get there. Thus, we focus on problem-solving during our cooperative planning for a project," Josie said.

"So, the strategy part is thinking through the best ways to solve the problems needed to successfully complete the project?" Anya asked.

"And the problem-solving strategy is to fill the gap between what you know and what you will need to learn!" Jake grinned.

"That's right," Josie said. *"And we identify that problem-solving gap by looking at the project objectives, figuring out what problems we need to solve to achieve those objectives, and lining up the resources we will need to accomplish the problem-solving."*

"Sooo... it's all about problem-solving," Jake trailed off.
"And sharing what you have learned," Anya added.
Josie paused for a moment and smiled. *"I believe you two will fit in very well here."*

***

Brains

While Neil Anderthal is trying to get his shrinking team to do more, Josie Wang is onboarding two new team members and orienting them to a new way of working. She is coaching them to become wisdom workers. Josie wants Jake and Anya to see themselves differently as part of this process. She wants them to take on a new perspective about how they bring value to their team and organization.

Josie is coaching Jake and Anya to believe that creating new knowledge and sharing it is how they bring value to their team, organization, and, ultimately, their clients. She wants them to realize her challenge – and their challenge, too – is to organize themselves, leverage technology, and work in a way that accelerates problem-solving.

Josie explains to Jake and Anya the importance of collaborative leadership in their teams to accelerate problem-solving. She ensures they know she facilitates cooperative planning to bring together everything about a project so the team can identify what problems must be solved to complete the project. Josie wants Jake and Anya to appreciate why she delegates control to the team members, so they have the most flexibility to achieve the needed learning. She also ensures Jake and Anya know that sharing what they have learned is critically essential. She is already working on instilling reciprocity in them.

Josie also begins coaching Jake and Anya on leveraging artificial intelligence. She aims to grow their brains by using technology to enhance their cognitive abilities, accelerate problem-solving, and foster innovation. Josie explains that it's a meaningful way to accelerate the problem-solving needed to complete a project. She outlines how her team members use technology to extend their cognitive abilities to reason about data and information, make conclusions, and use the implications to develop solutions for the problems that stand in their way. Josie wants them to envision themselves as having extended cognitive abilities and take the responsibility that comes with it.

Finally, Josie coaches Jake and Anya on why they should – individually and with other team members – develop a strategy for achieving the problem-solving needed to complete a project successfully. She stresses that their problem-solving strategy should be done upfront in the initial project planning to define project objectives, identify what problem-solving is needed to achieve those objectives, and determine the resources necessary to accomplish the problem-solving.

Josie is not only building skills with Jake and Anya. She is changing their perceptions of themselves, their teams, their organization, and their clients. On this day, she wanted them to walk away from the meeting with the idea they had more brains than they thought they had.

Key Actions for Increasing Organizational Intelligence

Grow Their Brains

- Employ Collaborative Leadership
- Leverage Artificial Intelligence
- Follow a Learning Strategy

Chapter 12

Grow Their Courage

"Did you hear about Jackie and Jim?" Sean shouted in a whisper.

"No, don't tell me they have also left the team," Patty said.

"Okay, I won't tell you," Sean said quietly.

"Alright, where did they go?" Patty asked.

"They went to a new project on Josie Wang's team," Sean said.

"I wonder if she's got a room for me?" Patty mused.

The door opened and in walked Dr. Anderthal. His pace was average but looked slow for him. "Today, let's see what's left to do to close out the two remaining projects."

Everyone noticed his voice seemed lower – subdued.

"Are you okay?" Patty asked. "We heard about Jackie and Jim going to Josie Wang's team."

Dr. Anderthal straightened up. "Of course, I'm okay. Let's get started on how we are going to finish the reporting on those projects without them."

You could have heard a pin drop as the binders were quietly opened.

***

"Hi, Jake and Anya. Come on into my office," Josie said.

"We heard Jackie and Jim are coming over to the team," Jake said with a little hesitation.

"That's right. I think they will be a good addition to our team. It looks like I will be having more onboarding meetings. Now, let's get to this week's topics. Let's start by talking about how we encourage each other to take on leadership responsibilities."

"Okay, but isn't leadership different than just being a worker?" Jake asked.

"It is, and it isn't," Josie said. "We all collaborate as workers on a team. So, in a sense, working on a team and being the leader of the team are the same. But you are also right that while serving as the team leader, you are taking more responsibility for the team's success."

DOI: 10.4324/9781003506591-17

Jake and Anya looked puzzled.

"Look," Josie said, "it all comes down to confidence. And the only way to build confidence for leading others is to practice. That means actually leading some efforts."

"I think for some people, leading others is hard to do," Jake said. "I know for me, and I would rather just do my part and let someone else oversee the whole project."

"Most of us are that way," Josie said. "But for us to have an effective team, we all must do our share of leadership. For wisdom workers, learning and leadership come with the territory."

"So how do we get the confidence to lead?" Anya asked.

"We build it together," Josie said. "First, we let you work as a team member. We allow you to build confidence in your ability to solve problems and create new knowledge to share."

"And that means leveraging artificial intelligence to expand our abilities for knowledge creation," said Jake.

"That's right," Josie said. "And artificial intelligence can also help us lead. Think about Socrates Digital® on budgeting and scheduling for our team projects. My leader, Ajay, our team members, and even our clients can access it and ask questions – just as if they were talking with me. Socrates Digital® is available 24/7, which allows our stakeholders to access needed information about any project while I'm working on other things."

"Which would also help us when we start leading an effort," Anya said thoughtfully.

"That's right," Josie said. "And I will help you set up Socrates Digital® for your budgets and schedules. So, you won't be on your own when we give you a chance to lead an effort. But do you remember the first thing we strive for in our team?"

"Do you mean that we strive to have a high level of psychological safety?" Jake asked.

"Yes, that's right" Josie nodded. "We will give you room to grow into the responsibilities of leadership. And that includes failing."

Jake and Anya looked at each other.

"What's wrong?" Josie asked.

"Well...," Jake said with a look of dismay. "We haven't had much chance to fail – yet alone lead in our previous group."

"That's fine," Josie said with a smile. "You'll get the chance to do both here."

Josie paused before saying, "You see, leadership is so important in our wisdom economy that we want you to start thinking about how you will become good at it – before you have done any of it."

"Why is leadership more important in the wisdom economy?" Anya asked.

"It's because of what we make," Josie said. "When we used to make things, the leader would simply ensure it got made. But now, since our team members bring value to our clients by creating new knowledge, we need to take great care to facilitate its creation. That means someone needs to 'shepherd' the process to ensure that everything is in place for problem-solving and knowledge creation to happen."

"That's because in the wisdom economy, people plan with machines to solve problems and machines work the plan," Jake said.

"That's right," Josie said. "And we want you to start now to see yourself as a leader."

"And it starts with having confidence in our abilities to create knowledge?" Anya asked.

"Yes, and we need to ensure we provide enough psychological safety for you to gain the leadership experience you will need to be successful," Josie said. "And we want you to get good at it so you can become a mentor to others as they join the team."

"So, they can become good leaders, too!" Jake said.

"That's the idea," Josie said with a smile.

"Now, let's talk about striving to do the right thing," Josie said. "On this team, we work hard to develop a culture so you can dare to do the right thing for yourself, team, and our stakeholders."

"This is honestly and stuff like that, right?" Jake asked.

"Yes, it's stuff like that," Josie said with a smile. "We want you to realize we now work in a strongly networked world. It's critical for you and everyone to know you endeavor to do the right thing."

"Why is it more important than, say, 20 years ago?" Anya asked.

"Because 20 years ago, people made things and one could easily judge the value of a thing that was made by evaluating it with objective criteria. But now, people create knowledge that becomes a solution to a problem, which in many cases is subjective since there are so many possible solutions. So, you want to be trusted as a person who does the right thing, which means your created knowledge is aimed at doing the right thing. It's hard to do at times, but it greatly increases the value of your work."

"So, that's why doing the right thing is so important for yourself, team, and stakeholders," Anya said.

"Yes, and it's my job to help create an environment so you can have the courage to do the right thing," Josie said.

Jake and Anya nodded.

"Given there are no further questions, let's get to the last topic for today," Josie said. "Let's now talk about sharing."

"You want one of my chips?" Jake asked as he pushed the bag toward Josie.

"No thanks, but if it were carrot cake, I'd be all over it!" Josie said with a laugh. "Knowledge sharing is one of the most misunderstood aspects of the wisdom economy."

"Why is that?" Jake asked. "I would think it would be simple. Since we are in the wisdom economy, we just pay people for sharing their knowledge."

"Well, that would work if we created knowledge on our own," Josie said. "But we actually create knowledge in teams. Since it's the synergy of people and intelligent machines working together, it's hard to identify what each team member has contributed."

"So, what is the answer?" Jake asked.

"Several things have to be in place," Josie said. "For one, we need a culture of 'first to share' for our team. That's my job to introduce and nurture."

"First to share?"

"The idea is to create the expectation that when one of us learns something, we naturally expect that person to share," Josie said. "So, we try to kick-start this idea of trusting new team members by sharing with them first."

"So, what does the new team member do with the shared knowledge?" Jake asked.

"Well, they may use it to complete a report or to generate new ideas for a product. It doesn't really matter. The expectation is that you document where the new knowledge came from."

"Like citing a book or other source?" Jake asked.

"That's right," Josie said.

"That's it? That's all there is to it?" Jake asked.

"I wish it were that easy," Josie said. "First, to share is simply to get things started. The most important thing to get people to share – and keep on sharing – is instilling the value for reciprocity."

"Recip....?" Jake asked.

"Reciprocity," Josie laughed. "It means if you share with me, then I'll share with you. What keeps it going is giving credit for the knowledge people have shared with you."

"Sounds a lot like kindergarten," Jake said with a grin.

"In some ways, it is," laughed Josie.

***

Courage

Neil Anderthal's leadership role is definitely in a death spiral. His team is voting with their feet and leaving him behind. He still doesn't get it. He is trying to get them to do more, but he doesn't know they are not supposed to be doing anything. The wisdom economy demands that they create new knowledge for the marketplace. And Josie Wang was right when she said you couldn't make people think or solve problems. It should be apparent to Neil Anderthal that he needs to spend less time controlling his people and more time stimulating their knowledge creation.

In the meantime, Josie Wang is moving on from coaching her new team members to increase their cognitive abilities to making them more courageous. Being courageous is an inherent value, but it requires skills for its application. Josie knows that, at their core, people want to be brave but sometimes don't know how to get there. For example, accepting the responsibility of leading a team takes courage. It also takes leadership skills to do an excellent job of it.

Josie begins coaching Jake and Anya on developing these skills by explaining why leadership is more critical in the wisdom economy than ever. She tells them that successful leadership starts with confidence in their abilities to create new knowledge. And she underscores that becoming a good leader takes practice. Josie makes sure they know they will have a high level of psychological safety while they are getting that practice. It will be okay to fail.

Since leadership is so essential, Josie wants Jake and Anya to know that when they become successful leaders, they will have to provide others with the opportunity to lead. Also, they will have to coach others on the skills required to become a successful leader.

Josie also continues coaching Jake and Anya, leveraging artificial intelligence in leadership roles. She reminds them how she uses artificial intelligence to provide access to expertise about the budgets and schedules for their team projects. She wants them to envision using artificial intelligence to extend their cognitive abilities and improve their leadership skills.

Next, Josie switches to the importance of doing the right thing. Josie coaches Jake and Anya on the value of being known for doing the right thing. She wants them to make this a core value in their work. She wants them to realize others will place a higher value on the knowledge they create if they are known for doing the right thing.

Finally, Josie coaches Jake and Anya on the principle of reciprocity. She lets them know the expectation is that they share what they have learned with the team and that the team will share what they have learned with them. Josie ensures Jake and Anya know that knowledge keeps flowing because everyone gets credit for contributing.

Key Actions for Increasing Organizational Intelligence

Grow Their Courage

- Embrace Opportunities to Lead Others
- Endeavor to Do the Right Thing
- Share What They Have Learned

Chapter 13

Grow Their Hearts

"Hi boss, do you have a moment?" Dr. Anderthal looked up from his desk to see Gerald at his door.

"Yes, come on in," Dr. Anderthal said with a sigh.

"I heard about...," Gerald began.

"My transfer?" Dr. Anderthal interrupted.

"Yeah," said Gerald. "I just wanted to come by and wish you the best of luck on your next assignment."

"Thanks, I'll need it," Dr. Anderthal said with another sigh. "You know, Gerald, I really appreciate that you came by to wish with me luck – thank you."

"You're welcome," Gerald said with a sad smile. "I gotta go – see you around."

After the door closed, Dr. Anderthal said quietly, "Not likely."

"Knock, knock" came from the door. "Come in," Dr. Anderthal said. "Everyone else is," he said under his breath.

"I hope I'm not disturbing you," Josie said.

"Oh, it's you – no, come right in," said Dr. Anderthal beginning to stand.

"No, don't get up, I just heard about your transition," Josie said with concern on her face.

"You mean my transfer to Siberia?"

"You mean you're being transferred to one of our field offices in the Midwest?"

"No, I really mean Siberia! Siberia, Russia," he said with a grimace. "Ajay wants me to lead a team that is field testing a new thermal suit for the United Nations."

"Oh," Josie said.

"So, I don't know if I'm coming back to Big Time," Dr. Anderthal said with a sigh.

"Well, read this before you decide if you want to come back," Josie said as she handed him a book.

"What's this?"

DOI: 10.4324/9781003506591-18

"It's a book that has helped me a lot in my leadership journey."

"Leadership in the Era of Personal AI: Growing Organizational Intelligence.[1] *Well, it looks like I'll have plenty of time to read it where I'm going,"* as he forced a little smile.

"Best of luck, Neil," Josie said as she put out her hand.

"Thanks, Josie," he said as he embraced her hand.

***

"Looks like Josie is late," Jake said. *"Let's just wait in the conference room outside her office."*

"It's not like her," Anya said.

Just then the hall door swung open. *"Sorry I'm late,"* Josie said. *"I made a little detour after my meeting with Ajay, and it took a little longer than I expected. Come on in."*

"No worries," Jake said. *"It's only a few minutes."*

"Carrot cake?" Jose asked with a smile.

"Yeah," Jake said as he grabbed a little paper plate.

"Not this time," Anya laughed. *"Last time I had two pieces."*

"Okay, and since this is our second-to-last onboarding meeting, let's talk about heart.," Josie said.

"Heart?" Jake wondered. *"Like the Tin Man getting a heart in the Wizard of Oz?"*

"Something like that," Josie said.

But then she became serious. *"I want you to know how important it is for you always to convey personal integrity, as it touches everything you do."*

"Yes, I can see why it would be important for interactions with your team members," Anya said.

"More than just your team members," Josie said. *"It's your clients and suppliers, too – everyone you connect with on a project."*

"Yeah," Jake said. *"I can see where it would be important for me to be trusted by all the people involved on my projects."*

Josie raised an eyebrow. *"It's more than just you."*

"What do you mean?" Jake said, obviously puzzled.

It's all that you create, as well," Josie said. *"When people on our team and outside interact with Socrates Digital® to access what you have learned, they are trusting you."*

"Oh," Jake said, thoughtfully.

"When you want to access Socrates Digital® that has access to other people's hard-earned knowledge, it's their trust in you that allows your access," Josie said.

Jake and Anya nodded.

"And it doesn't end there," Josie said. *"Your integrity has far-reaching influence. When you conduct a search for specific information, it may follow links to a Socrates Digital® that manages other people's private information, and sometimes, it belongs to people that you don't even know. Each time you will gain access to their information only if you are trusted. In the end, it's your integrity that will provide the access."*

"So personal integrity is more important than ever," Anya said thoughtfully.

"Indeed, it is," Josie said with a smile. *"Now, let's talk about something large."*

"Large?" Jake wondered.

"Yes," Josie said. *"Let's talk about something bigger than yourselves."*

Jake and Anya looked at each other.

"It's been my observation that people who believe in something bigger than themselves have a larger impact on their world than those who don't," Jose went on to say.

"Do you remember the time you came to me with a concern that your team leader was out to harm me?" Josie said.

"Yeah," Jake said.

"Do you remember what I was concerned about?" Josie asked.

"Yeah," Jake said. *"You seemed to be more concerned about everyone but yourself."*

"And now think back. Why did you come to me in particular?"

"Well, you were the one he was trying to get into trouble," Jake said.

"Is that the only reason?" Josie probed.

"No, not really. I'm guessing we came to you because we thought you'd try to do the right thing by everyone," Jake said.

"Do you think that I believe in something larger than myself that drives my actions?" Josie said.

"Yes, I would say that you also believe in the organization," Anya said thoughtfully.

"Does that make you trust me more?" Josie asked.

"Yes, it does," Anya said.

"Now, do you see why you should believe in something larger than yourself?

Jake and Anya nodded.

"And that brings us to the last topic for today," Josie said. *"Believing in something larger than yourself is the beginning. But to do the right thing, you must take on the best interests of those you lead."*

"So, that means you should look out for the team members in your group – like us," Jake said.

"That's right," Josie said. *"How did I look after the best interests of my team members in the situation Neil caused?"*

"You went to Socrates Digital® to see what Ajay asked it," Jake said.

"What do you think I was looking for?" Josie asked.

"If Socrates Digital® answered all Ajay's questions," Jake said.

"Who should I notify if Ajay didn't get the answers he needed to feel confident the project was on track?" Josie asked.

"Luke!" Anya burst out. "Of course, since he's in your team you would want him to know immediately if something was wrong. You were looking out for his best interests."

Josie smiled.

"And, you were looking out for Ajay, too," Jake said. "You could get him additional information if he didn't get what he needed from Socrates Digital®."

"And, you were looking out for your client, as well," Anya said slowly. "You wanted to make sure she was up to date on the project."

"But what about us," Jake said. "We weren't on your team then. Why were you looking after us?"

"At that time, you were part of our larger team," Josie said. "In looking after you, I was looking after the best interests of the organization. And, just as important, I was looking out for your best interests."

"And Dr. Anderthal," Anya asked. "Why did you look after his best interests?"

"Sometimes, you have to go the extra mile," Josie said with a smile. "You'll find it will do wonders for you."

***

Heart

Well, Neil Anderthal "has left the building."[2] However, we get a sense that he may still have a future. Josie senses that, too. She suspects he is a good person underneath it all. She also knows that a lot of leadership is learned. He may be modeling what he has seen as leadership. He may have learned to be "tough" to be respected. He may have learned to "do whatever it takes" to get ahead because everyone else is doing that, too. He also may have learned to believe in himself since that's the only thing that counts. He may only look out for his self-interest because he has learned that no one else will.

Thus, Josie gives him the book and another chance.

Now, Josie is moving from coaching her new team members from being more courageous to having more heart. She is helping Anya and Jake to understand that trust is the currency for knowledge sharing they need to nurture and grow. Josie begins by reminding them they are paid not for what they do but for the knowledge they create. In doing so, Josie points out they don't create knowledge alone. They create it with trusted others. Josie continues by coaching them in ways to build trust with others. She coaches them on conveying personal integrity, believing in something larger than themselves, and taking on the best interests of the ones they lead.

Josie easily convinces Jake and Anya to exhibit personal integrity to build trust with co-workers. The contrast of working with someone who does not convey personal integrity versus someone who does is striking. We can see that Josie has succeeded in getting Jake and Anya to take this value to heart.

Josie also continues coaching Jake and Anya on how their integrity is even more critical in the era of artificial intelligence. Josie points out that Socrates Digital® is an extension of themselves, and their value in the organization is directly related to their integrity. Josie also points out that their integrity provides access to other people's knowledge managed by Socrates Digital®. She wants Jake and Anya to know that their integrity is passed from machine to machine to gain access to other people's knowledge.

Josie has a more challenging time convincing Jake and Anya that believing in something larger than themselves will improve trust with others and make them more effective as wisdom workers. She decides to use her relationship with them to help them examine their feelings of trust in her. Josie progresses with this value because they can see how it increases their trust in her.

Finally, Josie puts it all together when she convinces Jake and Anya that taking on the best interests of those they lead is where the "rubber meets the road" in growing trust with others. They know Josie has their best interests in mind. And Jake and Anya see if they are to be as trusted as Josie, they will have to take on the best interests of those they lead. Without Josie telling them, Jake and Anya know they can't fake it; the people they lead will see if they are sincere in this core leadership principle. They will know the truth when they see it.

Key Actions for Increasing Organizational Intelligence

Grow Their Heart

- Convey Personal Integrity
- Believe in Something Greater than Themselves
- Take on Best Interests of Those They Lead

Notes

1 Yes, I know. It's a shameless promotion of my book. ☺
2 "Elvis has left the building." Reportedly, the phrase was first used by promoter Horace Lee Logan on December 15, 1956, near Shreveport, Louisiana, to plead with concert-goers to leave the concert hall since Elvis had already left. In the years since the phrase has been used to refer to anyone who has "gone on ahead" in some sense.

Chapter 14

Grow Their Leadership with AI

"Today, we talk about our last topic for onboarding," Josie said. "To become the best leaders that we can be in today's world, we need to leverage technology. For example, Socrates Digital®, can help with your personal growth as a leader."

"How is that?" Jake asked.

"On a personal level," we can think of becoming a great leader in the era of personal AI as a result of keeping the nine promises to ourselves," Josie said.

"What are the nine promises?" Anya asked.

Josie smiled and said, "We have been talking about them all along. Keep these promises and you will become a great leader in the Era of AI."

1 *"Employ Collaborative Leadership*
2 *Develop and Implement a Problem-Solving Strategy*
3 *Leverage Artificial Intelligence*
4 *Embrace Opportunities to Lead Others*
5 *Endeavor to Do the Right Thing*
6 *Share What I Have Learned*
7 *Convey Personal Integrity*
8 *Believe in Something Larger than Myself, and*
9 *Take on Best Interests of Those I Lead"*

"OK," Jake said. "So, how does Socrates Digital® help us keep these promises to ourselves?"

"Let's find out," Josie said with smile. "Socrates Digital®, I'm told that a fellow manager has said something about my project that is untrue. What should I do?"

Socrates Digital® responds with, "This situation touches on several of your promises, but most prominently, it seems to relate to:

Employ Collaborative Leadership: This promise involves working together with others, including resolving conflicts or misunderstandings in a constructive way.

DOI: 10.4324/9781003506591-19

Develop and Implement a Problem-Solving Strategy: This promise can guide you to systematically approach the situation, identify the misinformation, and find a solution.

Convey Personal Integrity: This promise is about maintaining your honesty and transparency, ensuring that your actions reflect your commitment to truth and ethical behavior.

Take on Best Interests of Those I Lead: This promise underscores the importance of safeguarding the morale and trust within your team, which can be affected by untrue statements about your project.

Given these promises, it sounds like you're grappling with how to maintain your personal integrity while also employing collaborative leadership to address the situation."

"Actually, I think it's more about Take on Best Interests of Those I Lead," Josie said.

Socrates Digital® continues with, "Understood, focusing on the promise to 'Take on the Best Interests of Those I Lead' frames this situation in the context of leadership and the impact on your team or project stakeholders. Addressing misinformation not only protects the integrity of the project but also the morale and trust of those involved.

Given this focus, let's explore this further:

Do you know any person or persons that would be hurt if you don't address the untrue statement about your project?"

"Yes, I'm afraid that my client, Heather Wilton of the CIA, could be hurt by this untruth," Josie replies.

"Thank you for sharing that. It's important to consider the impact of misinformation on stakeholders, especially in critical roles like Heather Wilton's at the CIA. Addressing this concern proactively can help maintain trust and credibility, Socrates Digital® continues.

"Do you have any evidence that Heather Wilton or the project will be negatively affected by this untrue statement?"

"Heather Wilton of the CIA asked last week if the budget or schedule had been changed for the project. I told her that the budget and schedule or budget has not changed during the last three months of the project," Josie said.

In response, Socrates Digital® said, "It sounds like Heather Wilton's inquiry about the budget or schedule changes could be related to the untrue statement made by your fellow manager. Her question indicates she might have heard something that led her to question the project's status, which aligns with your concern about potential harm due to misinformation.

Socrates Digital® continues, "What assumptions are you making about the situation?"

Josie responds with, "I'm going to assume that no harm was done to my client."

Socrates Digital® notes, "That's a positive assumption, focusing on the possibility that your client, Heather, has not been negatively impacted by the misinformation so far. This assumption allows you to approach the situation with a view toward clarification and reaffirmation rather than damage control."

Socrates Digital® asks, "Given this assumption, what would you conclude to do to correct the situation and keep your promise to take on the best interests of those you lead?"

"I conclude that the untruth did not harm my client," Josie responds.

Socrates Digital® comments, "Given your conclusion that the untruth did not harm your client, it sounds like you're leaning toward a proactive and clarifying approach rather than a reactive one. This approach can involve reinforcing the facts about the project's budget and schedule directly with Heather Wilton, ensuring she has accurate information and feels supported and valued in her role. Moving forward with this conclusion, what implications do you think your action of reinforcing the accurate project status and ensuring clear communication will have?"

Josie answers, "The implication is that my client didn't suffer any consequences for this unfortunate situation."

Socrates Digital® summarizes, "That's a constructive implication. By proactively addressing the situation and ensuring that your client, Heather Wilton, is working with the most accurate and up-to-date information, you're not only mitigating any potential confusion or concern she might have had but also strengthening the trust and transparency in your professional relationship. This action underscores your commitment to taking on the best interests of those you lead, including external stakeholders like clients."

"Now, let's see how Socrates Digital® can help with another promise we need to keep for becoming a great leader in the era of personal AI," Josie said.

"Socrates Digital®, I have two new reports that I want to integrate into our team. What should I do?"

Socrates Digital® responds, "Integrating new reports into your team, in a way that aligns with the narrative and values you've shared, most closely relates to the promise of Believe in Something Larger than Myself. This promise encompasses fostering a team culture that goes beyond individual achievements to embrace a shared mission or purpose. By focusing on this promise, your actions encourage team members to connect their personal goals with the broader objectives of the team and organization."

"Yes, I think that you are correct. It is about having them believe in something larger than themselves," Josie said. "What should I think about next?"

Socrates Digital® comes back, "With the focus on helping your new reports believe in something larger than themselves, the next steps involve reflection and action that both communicate and embody this value."

"Do you know any person or persons that would be hurt if you don't suc-cessfully integrate these new reports with this promise in mind? This question prompts you to think about the broader impact of successful integration, not just on the new reports, but on the entire team, your projects, and potentially the wider community your team serves," Socrates Digital® said.

Josie responds, "Yes, the new reports will be hurt if I don't successfully integrate them into our team."

"Recognizing that the new reports stand to be hurt if not successfully inte-grated underlines the importance of your actions. This awareness is the first step toward ensuring their successful integration, in alignment with the belief in something larger than themselves," Socrates Digital® said. "Do you have any evidence that the new reports will be negatively affected if they are not integrated with this promise in mind?"

"Yes, I have seen new members in a group not fully engaging in teamwork because they don't believe in the larger goal of the team," Josie said.

"Your observation highlights a critical aspect of team dynamics—when new members aren't fully aligned with or aware of the team's larger goals, their engagement and contribution can suffer. This can lead to a lack of cohesion and can ultimately impact the team's performance and morale," Socrates Digital® said. "What assumptions are you making about the situation? This question encourages you to examine any underlying be-liefs or expectations you have regarding the integration process and its challenges."

Josie answers, "I'm assuming that if I can explain what our larger goals are, they will start to believe in them."

"That's a positive and proactive assumption, focusing on the power of communication and shared goals to inspire belief and commitment. It reflects an understanding that clear articulation of your team's larger mission can be a key factor in fostering alignment and engagement among new team mem-bers," Socrates Digital® said. "Given this assumption, what would you con-clude to do to correct the situation and ensure the new reports start to believe in the larger goals of the team?"

"I conclude that explaining what our larger goals are as a team to my new reports is the best path forward," Josie, answers.

Socrates Digital® notes, "Great! Moving forward with the assumption that explaining the larger goals will help new reports believe in them is a good idea. What implications do you think your action of explaining and integrat-ing the larger goals will have?"

"I think that the new reports will believe in something bigger than them-selves and end up integrating with our team," Josie said.

Socrates Digital® summarizes, "That's an encouraging outlook. By ef-fectively communicating the larger goals and demonstrating how each team member contributes to these objectives, you're not just integrating new reports into the team; you're also instilling a sense of purpose and belonging. This approach can lead to several positive implications:

Increased Team Cohesion: When everyone is aligned with a common purpose, it fosters a sense of unity and teamwork. Team members are more likely to support each other and work collaboratively toward shared goals.

Enhanced Motivation and Engagement: Believing in something larger than oneself can be a powerful motivator. It provides a deeper reason for coming to work each day and puts daily tasks into a larger context.

Higher Job Satisfaction: Employees who feel their work has meaning and contributes to a greater good tend to have higher job satisfaction. This can lead to lower turnover rates and a more committed workforce.

Positive Organizational Culture: Cultivating a belief in larger goals contributes to a positive organizational culture, where values and purpose drive actions. This can attract like-minded individuals to your team and organization, further strengthening your culture.

Broader Impact: By focusing on goals that extend beyond individual achievements, your team can make a significant impact on the broader community or industry. This can enhance your organization's reputation and lead to new opportunities.

"Remember," Socrates Digital® continues. "Integrating new reports with an emphasis on believing in something larger than themselves requires consistent effort and reinforcement. Keep the dialogue open, celebrate contributions to shared goals, and continue to lead by example. This sustained effort can transform individual team members' commitment into a collective force that drives both team success and personal fulfillment."

"Thanks," Josie said with a smile. "And that, Jake and Anya, is how Socrates Digital® can help you keep these nine promises and become a great leader in the Era of personal AI."

***

Leadership with AI

This conversation revolves around the role Socrates Digital® can play in fostering leadership qualities and addressing professional challenges in the era of personal AI. Josie introduces the concept of becoming a great leader by following nine promises, which she believes are pivotal for successful leadership in the context of AI. These promises include employing collaborative leadership, developing problem-solving strategies, leveraging AI, embracing leadership opportunities, striving for ethical behavior, sharing knowledge, maintaining integrity, believing in a cause greater than oneself, and prioritizing the interests of those led.

The discussion progresses with an example where Josie seeks advice from Socrates Digital® on handling misinformation spread by a colleague about her project, potentially harming her client's interests. This scenario ties back to the nine promises, highlighting the importance of integrity, collaborative problem-solving, and prioritizing the team or project stakeholders' best interests. Socrates Digital® suggests a thoughtful approach to address the misinformation, emphasizing maintaining integrity and trust within the team and with external stakeholders, like clients.

Furthermore, Josie seeks guidance from Socrates Digital® about integrating two new reports into her team. Socrates Digital® suggests that this task aligns with the promise of believing in something larger than oneself, underlining the necessity of fostering a team culture that values collective goals over individual achievements. Josie and Socrates Digital® discuss strategies to ensure the successful integration of new team members by aligning them with the team's broader objectives, thus enhancing team cohesion, motivation, job satisfaction, and the overall organizational intelligence.

Throughout the conversation, Socrates Digital® acts as a guide, helping Josie navigate leadership challenges by applying the nine promises.[1] This discussion illustrates the potential of AI tools like Socrates Digital® in supporting leaders to make decisions that are ethical, collaborative, and aligned with the broader goals of their teams and organizations, ultimately contributing to personal growth as a leader in the age of AI.

Key Actions for Increasing Organizational Intelligence

Grow More Leadership with AI

- Grow Their Brains
- Grow Their Courage
- Grow Their Heart

Note

1 The responses provided by Socrates Digital® in this conversation were created by configuring prompts for ChatGPT, a large language model, to develop a Socratic problem-solving application.

Part 5

Organizational Intelligence Requires Personal Growth

Chapter 15

Grow More Brains

Chapters 15–18 are about you. They give you an opportunity to plot your own path for your future. This is your chance to become a wisdom worker and learn how to lead others like you.

These chapters describe nine promises to yourself you will have to keep if you are going to become a wisdom worker and grow organizational intelligence in your own place of work. The promises are grouped into three categories. This chapter, Chapter 15, presents the promises to Have More Brains. Chapter 16 presents the promises to Have More Courage. And Chapter 17 presents the promises to Have More Heart. Each chapter has a summary of the promises for the chapter. All nine promises are listed in Chapter 18 – the end of this book.

More Brains

Employ Collaborative Leadership

My first job after graduate school was with a research and development (R&D) group focused on creating intelligent human-computer interfaces. I soon became acquainted with more people in the R&D community and began working with several teams on different projects. These teams had what I would later call a collaborative leadership model, and I found that the emphasis was on something other than getting things done. The idea of getting paid to create knowledge rather than doing something was an unusual job for the time. But a lot has happened in the workplace since then. In the wisdom economy, we are all R&D workers. The jobs where people are paid to do things are disappearing rapidly. People are now paid to create new knowledge, whereas it's up to machines to act on that knowledge.

Promise Yourself

Promise yourself you will facilitate cooperative planning, delegate control to team members to allow them flexibility for accelerating problem-solving and improve knowledge sharing by instilling reciprocity in your team members.

DOI: 10.4324/9781003506591-21

Utilize a Problem-Solving Strategy

After I started my own company, we began to use a problem-solving strategy as part of our planning for new projects. We started with the end goal of a new project in mind. In other words, we asked ourselves, "What would a 'breakthrough' project look like?" After identifying what success would look like, we considered what we knew would allow us to complete that breakthrough project successfully. For us, this priority placed problem-solving first and foremost in planning new work.

Next, we would ask, "What problems do we need to solve to make that breakthrough project successful?" The next question would be, "How feasible is it to solve these problems?" Another question is, "How much risk is there in undertaking this problem-solving – for example, do we have to learn too many unknown concepts or examine too many assumptions?" Finally, we would ask ourselves, "Do we have enough time and resources to learn what we need to learn?"

If we could answer all these questions satisfactorily with a high level of confidence, we would lay out a plan for accessing resources and develop a schedule for completing the problem-solving we need to do to achieve a successful project. Our finished problem-solving strategy was a plan for knowledge creation – the very thing we were paid to do.

Promise Yourself

Promise yourself that you will develop a strategy for achieving the problem-solving needed to complete a project successfully.

Leverage Artificial Intelligence

In my first job with the R&D group, I developed a "paper-based" knowledge repository in my filing cabinet on various technologies and research topics. My team members, manager, and clients would come to me asking if I had information on a particular topic. The information I had collected often became the basis for a new project. I realized my knowledge about various matters was more significant than what I carried around in my head. (There is a whole field of study on this. See, for example, Salomon's collection of essays on distributed cognition by various authors.)[1] My ability to create something new from the information stored in my file cabinet was of real value to my team, company, and clients. This book shows how to leverage artificial intelligence to expand the information available to you and use it to create new knowledge.

Promise Yourself

Promise you will use technology to extend your cognitive abilities, accelerate problem-solving, and foster innovation.

I Promise Myself to Grow More Brains

- Employ Collaborative Leadership
- Develop and Implement a Problem-Solving Strategy
- Leverage Artificial Intelligence

Note

1 G. Salomon, *Distributed Cognitions* (New York: Cambridge University Press, 1996).

Chapter 16

Grow More Courage

This chapter presents the promises to Have More Courage. At the end of the chapter, there is a summary of these promises. Chapter 17, the last chapter of the book, lists all nine promises.

More Courage

Embrace Opportunities to Lead Others

I worked for several R&D groups and on many projects across the first company that I worked for. However, I never thought much about leadership. I worked for many supervisors, most of whom made leadership look easy. They employed many of the behaviors described in this book. Later, I utilized many of those behaviors when I had my own company. It seemed so common sense to me that I never thought I would have to teach people explicitly how to lead. I thought they could absorb it as I had. But later in my career, I realized, "No, most people can't just absorb leadership skills – they need to be taught." Hopefully, this book has shown you how to lead. Now, it's time for you to practice doing it.

Promise Yourself

Promise yourself you will embrace opportunities to lead others. You will begin by seeking opportunities to build your confidence in leading efforts on your team. After gaining confidence in your abilities to lead, you will provide opportunities for others to learn to lead. Finally, you will mentor those individuals to develop their leadership skills further.

Endeavor to Do the Right Thing

In my own company, we had a situation where our client thought we had agreed to include a feature in the software under the current contract. We had not mentioned that feature in our written contract. However, our project leader told the

DOI: 10.4324/9781003506591-22

client we would include that feature in our delivery. Of course, developing that feature would cost us money we couldn't charge the client. It's easy to do the right thing when it doesn't cost you anything, but it's hard to do if there's a price. However, without hesitation, we decided to do the right thing, provide the feature under the contract, and absorb the costs – meaning we made less money.

Notwithstanding, in the long run, we showed our client we were a company intent on doing the right thing, eventually leading to more contracts with that client. However, I made it a point to impress on our project manager – and all our leaders – that we must be careful about what we promise our clients. It doesn't matter if it's written down, as we will be on the hook for that promise because we are a company that strives to do the right thing. It turns out that doing the right thing is best for everyone involved.

Promise Yourself

Promise yourself you will endeavor to do the right thing for yourself, your team, your organization, and the other project stakeholders.

Share Knowledge

At the beginning of my career, I worked in a group with an amazing software engineer. He was in high demand. He worked on our projects and helped other groups with their issues. Mostly, he would write code himself to solve specific problems that had stalled projects. He was generally so busy that he didn't have time to teach anyone how to solve these problems themselves. And when raises came around, he would get a big one. Obviously, he was paid for what he did, and everyone knew it. It was also obvious he wasn't paid for sharing what he learned.

On a personal level, our software engineer was quite happy showing people how he did his work. However, as he planned his day, he put effort into doing things because that was what the company paid him to do. He was honest about the value of "giving a day's work for a day's pay."

If we could have given him truth serum, he would have said that sharing what he knows with people is a great idea, and he wished he could do more of it. But he also knew the company was paying him to get things done, so that's where he put his effort.

His hard work paid off years later, and he was promoted to a Technical Fellow position. At the company, this is the highest position for an engineer. His job involved researching and developing new engineering methods and consulting on big projects.

Guess what happened to his work? He moved from doing things for his pay to creating and sharing new knowledge. He was highly successful as a Technical Fellow and was highly sought after for his expertise on big projects.

The lesson here is that he was a sharing person before. It's just that people – including him – thought the best way for him to give a day's work for a day's pay was to do the work. As the wisdom economy has evolved, many recognize that the most outstanding value he can provide his company is to create and share new knowledge.

This same thing is happening to all of us in the wisdom economy. Thus, the most outstanding value that you can provide your organization is creating and sharing new knowledge.

Promise Yourself

Promise yourself you will share the knowledge you have created, give credit for the knowledge others have created, and instill reciprocity of knowledge sharing in your organization.

I Promise Myself to Grow More Courage

- Embrace Opportunities to Lead Others
- Endeavor to Do the Right Thing
- Share What I Have Learned

Chapter 17

Grow More Heart

This chapter presents the promises to Have More Heart. At the end of the chapter, there is a summary of these promises. And, again, Chapter 18, the last chapter of the book, lists all nine promises.

More Heart

Convey Personal Integrity

When I started my company, we had just entered into a large contract with a big client. We had to hire people in a hurry to have time to fulfill the work outlined in the contract. We didn't have time to train people for the work, so they would need to be ready to do it when we hired them. Thus, we emphasized skills as the main criteria for hiring. That ended up being a mistake I vowed never to make again. After hiring several highly skilled new employees, we had misunderstandings and miscommunications with our big client that made us look like we needed more ethical practices. It took much effort to straighten it out, and I felt it damaged our good name.

Afterward, I promised never to make technical skills the primary criterion for hiring again.

As a result, we decided to prioritize integrity in our hiring practices and then look for commitment and motivation, followed by technical skills. We could always provide the means for people to learn the necessary technical skills. However, personal integrity is something that must come from deep inside people. No one can give it to them.

Promise Yourself

Promise yourself you will tell the truth, give a day's work for a day's pay, and guard your character.

DOI: 10.4324/9781003506591-23

Believe in Something Larger than Yourself

I once worked for a boss solely focused on advancing his career. Like Neil Anderthal in this book, his only motivation was to get ahead. As a result, he continually pushed people who reported to him to do things that would make him look good. Because of this, I spent most of my time and effort reacting to "emergencies," which, if satisfactorily resolved, would make him seem responsive to his supervisor. Working in this way made me feel I was wasting much of my time – that I wasn't using my time in the company's best interests. I moved to another position as soon as I could. There, I found myself working for a leader who believed in our organization, our mission, and how what we were doing was something larger than ourselves. It was like the difference between night and day.

Promise Yourself

Promise yourself you will believe in something larger than yourself, work for an organization that believes in something larger than the organization and align your personal goals accordingly.

Take on Best Interests of Those You Lead

The boss I described above, who wanted me to focus on his best interests, did not have my best interests in mind. The leader who believed in something larger than herself also looked after my best interests. As you might expect, believing in something greater than yourself and caring for the best interests of others are related.

There was a world of difference between these two worlds of supervision. In the first situation, when working for a boss who does not have our best interests in mind, most of us make minimal effort to satisfy the value of "give a day's work for a day's pay." We won't volunteer for anything more. In the second situation, when working with a leader with our best interests in mind, we are willing to go beyond expectations and make extraordinary efforts when required for success. I know I have done that for a leader who had my best interests in mind. Looking after the best interests of those you lead is the most essential value of effective leadership – so much so that I follow it passionately.

When you look after the best interests of those you lead, they will, in turn, look out for your best interests and the best interests of the organization. In the wisdom economy, where you must enlist the assistance of those you lead to create new knowledge, it is the "secret sauce" of leadership!

Promise Yourself

Promise yourself you will take on the best interests of your team members, organization, and project stakeholders.

I Promise Myself to Grow More Heart

- Exhibit Personal Integrity
- Believe in Something Larger than Myself
- Take on Best Interests of Those I Lead

Chapter 18

Grow a Better Future

"Hi, it's great to see you!" Anya said.

"And it's great to see you, too," Josie said with a smile. "It's been a while since we've had lunch together."

"A lot has happened," Anya said.

"Tell me about your new R&D Company. How's it going?"

"Well, start-up is always hard, but we just got another contract, and we are looking to expand,"

"And I hear you have a new VP – someone I know," Josie said.

"That's right," Anya said with a smile. "Neil Anderthal, of all people. Who would have thought I would hire him?"

"I hear he's a different person these days," Josie said between bites.

"He is, indeed! I think those Russians made an impression on him."

"I heard they beat him up and threw him out of the building," Jose said.

"That's what Neil told me. It was then that he started reading the book you gave him. You know, his dad is a pastor and Neil was reminded of the Golden Rule every day when he was growing up. I think he just got off on the wrong foot, leadership-wise. He was taught that bullying people was the best way to get results from them."

"Yeah, I remember," Josie said.

"You wouldn't know he's the same person today. For example, he's on-boarding two new people to our company today. And you should see how he leads the R&D teams. You would've thought he invented collaborative leadership! His wife tells me he uses it at home with their kids!"

"That's good to hear," Josie said. "I always thought Neil was a good person underneath it all, and that he had a lot of talent."

"He does," Anya said. "He uses technology to increase his brain power and mentor others on how to do it, too. When you combine his expanded intelligence with his collaborative leadership, he's able to lead our company to new heights." She paused, thoughtfully. "And you, Josie, how do you like being CEO of Big Time R&D?"

DOI: 10.4324/9781003506591-24

"I really like it. I feel I have the opportunity to use my leadership skills to take us to a new level."

"That's great. I'm happy for you."

"And I for you."

Anya paused for a moment. "You know, our company is carving out space in the R&D world that is not in competition with Big Time. We complement Big Time very well in some technical areas. We could work together on many projects."

"I would like that very much," Josie said with a smile.

***

Now It's Up to You

Now that you have finished reading this book, you will navigate your professional world with a renewed perspective on the importance of organizational intelligence. This wisdom goes beyond the traditional workplace, encouraging a holistic understanding of our interconnected world.

Your foundation will be built on timeless human values: unwavering personal integrity, a commitment to larger causes, and an innate desire to prioritize collective well-being. The Golden Rule will be more than a philosophy; it will dictate your every interaction.

With the rise of the wisdom economy, forward-thinking organizations now recognize and seek the richness of these values. They understand that trusting and valuing their workforce is paramount in our increasingly complex world. And in this landscape, your unique blend of ethics and knowledge will be highly sought after.

Empowered by this enlightenment, you'll be impervious to manipulative or dominating leadership. Instead, you'll follow leaders who reflect your attributes: intellect, bravery, and heartfelt compassion.

Furthermore, as technology continues to evolve, you'll seamlessly collaborate with intelligent machines, using them not just as tools but as partners in the journey of knowledge creation and dissemination.

Embrace this new perspective with confidence. You have matured into a paradigm-shifting wisdom worker and leader.

Nine Promises to Myself

Grow More Brains

- Employ Collaborative Leadership
- Develop and Implement a Problem-Solving Strategy
- Leverage Artificial Intelligence

Grow More Courage

- Embrace Opportunities to Lead Others
- Endeavor to Do the Right Thing
- Share What I Have Learned

Grow More Heart

- Convey Personal Integrity
- Believe in Something Larger than Myself
- Take on Best Interests of Those I Lead

The technology described in this book is already here. For more information about the author and how to increase your organizational intelligence, go to www.marksalisbury.com.

Index

Note: *Italic* page numbers refer to figures and page numbers followed by "n" denote endnotes.

Printed in the United States
by Baker & Taylor Publisher Services